Pit Lasses

MINING HERITAGE SERIES

Other books in the series:

Pit Lasses

Women and Girls in Coalmining c.1800–1914

DENISE BATES

MINING HERITAGE
SERIES

Series Editor
Brian Elliott

Wharncliffe Books

DEDICATION

For Christopher, David and Andrew

First Published in Great Britain in 2012 by
Wharncliffe Books
an imprint of
Pen and Sword Books Ltd
47 Church Street
Barnsley
South Yorkshire
S70 2AS

Copyright © Denise Bates 2012

ISBN: 978-1-84563-155-2

Typeset by Concept, Huddersfield.

Printed and bound in England by CPI Group (UK) Ltd,
Croydon, CR0 4YY.

Pen & Sword Books Ltd incorporates the imprints of
Pen & Sword Aviation, Pen & Sword Family History,
Pen & Sword Maritime, Pen & Sword Military,
Pen & Sword Discovery, Wharncliffe Local History,
Wharncliffe True Crime, Wharncliffe Transport,
Pen & Sword Select, Pen & Sword Military Classics,
Leo Cooper, The Praetorian Press, Remember When,
Seaforth Publishing and Frontline Publishing.

For a complete list of Pen & Sword titles please contact
PEN & SWORD BOOKS LIMITED
47 Church Street
Barnsley
South Yorkshire
S70 2BR
England
E-mail: enquiries@pen-and-sword.co.uk
Website: www.pen-and-sword.co.uk

Contents

Introduction

Let it not be said that the House was jealous of the rights of
property but that it was not equally jealous of the rights of poverty.

Earl of Galloway in the House of Lords, 14 July 1842,
during the second reading of the Mines Bill

Pit Lasses was inspired by my great, great, great, great grandmother,
Rebecca Whitehead, who is listed as a miner on the 1841 census, a year
before women were banned from working underground. In May 1842,
a Royal Commission of Inquiry into the condition of children working
in mines ignited a public scandal about women and girls hauling coals
underground whilst naked to the waist, losing all vestiges of decency and
modesty, and incapable of running a home or bringing up their children in
good ways.

Keen to understand more about what Rebecca might have experienced,
I delved into a report produced by the Royal Commission. As I read
the individual statements given by women and girls who worked underground, I realised that their evidence did not support the negative picture,
which had been drawn in 1842 and handed down the generations. I began
to trace some witnesses to the 1841 census, hoping that their individual
family circumstances would provide context to their words and to the
Royal Commission report.

Within a few weeks interest had become fascination. Every new discovery raised another question and as I followed these through an entirely
different perspective on the life of a female miner in the nineteenth century
began to emerge.

Translating fascination into a researched book requires discipline and
commitment. In interpreting nineteenth-century female coal miners for a
twenty-first century audience, I have received an exceptional amount of
help and support from many people. Without this, *Pit Lasses* would never
have been written.

First and foremost my thanks go to my husband, sons, mother, mother-
in-law and family friend and fellow historian, Rachel Anchor, who have
provided inspiration, encouragement and practical assistance. Their
interest, comments and willingness to understand the lives of the women
and girls who have invaded my conversations and occupied my time for
the last eighteen months has been exceptional.

My editor at Pen and Sword, Brian Elliott, championed my book proposal from the moment he received it for evaluation. Brian has remained

constantly accessible and very supportive throughout the research and writing process.

Mining historian Ian Winstanley developed the Coal Mining History Resources Centre's website. His generosity in making his own research and a range of primary texts about coal mining, freely available to anyone with an interest in the subject is a great service to research. Being able to study evidence obtained by the Royal Commission at home in my spare time was the catalyst that sparked my own further research.

Part of my research involved trying to identify what happened to some of the female miners after 1842. I have been fortunate in making contact with descendants or relatives of some of the witnesses who have provided information and, in one instance, a family photograph of a female miner in old age, which is included as an illustration.

A number of librarians and archivists have assisted with queries. Richard Temple at the Senate House Library, London, Ellie Swithinbank at the Scottish Mining Museum and staff at the National Mining Museum in Wakefield supplied valuable details. I have been made very welcome in my visits to Leeds library and Barnsley library and cannot praise too highly the staff of the local studies library in Ashton-under-Lyne, who have supported me throughout the hours of research I undertook there.

Illustrations have been obtained from a variety of sources and I am grateful to my husband for his help in locating some of the places associated with the Inquiry. Brian Elliott and the Coal Mining History Resources Centre, provided images from their own collections.

A very special thank you is given to my mother-in-law, Margaret Bates. She has been a talented amateur artist all her life. After hearing details provided by some Commission witnesses she produced interpretations of their evidence, sketched from her own imagination.

Coal mining is an industry whose characteristics are regional rather than national. In writing a book which covers several regions I have encountered local vocabulary. The term for moving coals underground varied from district to district and depended upon whether the coals were pushed, pulled or carried. When writing in a generic context I have used the Yorkshire terms, hurrying and hurrier to describe this activity or the workers undertaking it. When referring to the activity in a particular place or to a named person I have used the term that applied in the district or the description of the individual's work given in the Commission's report. A glossary of mining terms is included at the back of this book, after the Appendices.

The source materials drawn upon are mainly nineteenth-century records; reports from Royal Commissions, census returns and newspaper reports. Research in these primary sources has been supplemented by some modern studies, which illuminate the context of the nineteenth century or its coal mining industry.

❋   ❋   ❋

I hope that this approach has peeled away the misconceptions that have persisted about female miners for 170 years and revealed them as the decent, capable girls and women they undoubtedly were.

The main coalfields of Britain during the nineteenth century. (Brian Elliott collection)

CHAPTER 1

King Coal
Women and mining 1800 – 1830

I canna say that I like the work well for I am obliged to do it: it is
horse work.

Agnes Kerr, 15, coal bearer

Coal, the black as night source of nineteenth-century Britain's heat, power
and industrial wealth is a carboniferous rock that formed over many
millions of years. Compressed under its own weight, rotting vegetation
gradually transformed into a mineral capable of fuelling the rise of an
industrial nation. The earth's ever-moving crust split, tore and folded the
special mineral until in some places it ran in deep, thick, horizontal layers,
in others it undulated in thin, fractured bands and where an ice-age had
ground the concealing layers away it rested on the surface exposed to the
elements.

How the combustible properties of this hard, black rock were discovered
is unknown but geological evidence shows that it has been mined for many
centuries. Shallow, bell-shaped pits where coal outcropped on the surface
were worked by all able-bodied members of the family as part of a mixed
household economy, which included growing crops, raising livestock,
spinning, weaving and working with wood.

When land ownership became concentrated in the hands of a small
number of noble or powerful families they laid claim to the rich crops that
could be harvested from beneath the surface. Where seams were thick coal
mining became an organised industry. Experts were brought in to sink
shafts and install the machinery, which made it possible to raise coal out
of the ground in bulk. Workers hired from within the local community
went underground to cut and move the coal. The artist Thomas Harrison
Hair produced drawings that show that in the early nineteenth century
coal extraction around Newcastle and Durham was a sophisticated and
extensive industry.

❋   ❋   ❋

The involvement of women in early commercial mining is shrouded in
mystery. It is unlikely that they ever formed more than a small fraction of

the workforce or that their role was other than as an assistant to a male worker, often their husband. A woman's task was twofold: to move the rocks that her man had loosened; and to represent his interest at the pit-head by ensuring that everything she carried to the surface was credited to his account.

By 1780, females are reported to have ceased mining in the north east of England. As factories proliferated and demanded more and more coal to power manufacturing, owners of pits which had thick, extensive seams identified the factors which enabled them to increase output. Using large trucks to convey hewn coal from the face to the shaft was more productive than moving it in small tubs. It was more cost effective to employ the greater strength of an adolescent male or a couple of boys working together to push the heavier trucks. Around the turn of the century it is likely that the number of females working underground silently peaked and began to decline.

When the sub-Commissioners for the Children's Employment Commission collected their evidence in 1841 they interviewed a number of older miners. From these statements it is possible to catch a glimpse of a female's role in mining communities from around 1800.

By the beginning of the century women were welcomed only in the places where owners were not interested in increased production. Sometimes this was because owners were scraping an income from their mines and had no money to invest in improving underground conditions to enable larger trucks to be used. Sometimes the seams were thin or of poor quality coal and the cost of improving them would not be recouped by any additional output.

Bad pits were often found in places where seams were thin and difficult to work. Owners needed women to work in them because there were some jobs that males would not do. Carrying coal on their backs was one task. The bearers who brought the coal out of primitive pits in Scotland were virtually all female.

William Muckle explained that in the 1790s early marriage had been essential for a Scottish miner as otherwise all the profits of his work went to pay the bearer and he had nothing to live on after buying his tools and candles. Other witnesses referred to the fact that a miner selected a wife based not on liking or affection but because she was a sturdy lass who would carry coal on her back for him. They were restricted in their choice to miners' daughters as girls not brought up in mining families refused to accept the drudgery.

For a mining lassie the choice was equally stark. She could accept an offer of marriage and carry coals for her husband or she could continue to work underground carrying them for her father. Girls who had grown up working in a pit were not chosen as wives by anyone other than a miner as they were considered capable of nothing beyond the drudgery of carrying coal.

For several centuries Scottish miners had been tied to the land, unable to move and take work elsewhere without their employers' permission, until the practice was finally abolished in 1799. This meant that inter-marriage involving just a few families was common in many villages. Some Scottish doctors thought that generations of such marriages were causing inherited health problems within mining villages by the mid-nineteenth century. Deterioration caused by the gene-pool becoming restricted was not a point that was discussed by the sub-Commissioners but it is known that this can happen.

The opinions of a few doctors at a time when medical science was in its infancy cannot be treated as evidence that problems were occurring in mining communities and if they were environmental factors would have to be examined as a potential cause. Whether the widely reported refusal of other types of worker to consider marriage with colliers' families hinted at deeper concerns than whether a woman could keep a decent home or whether she was prepared to move coal is unknown.

✻　✻　✻

In all areas of the country where females worked underground, work in the pits was a family affair. Owners usually hired workers on a sub-contract basis, with miners undertaking to produce a certain quantity of coal and deliver it to an agreed place. Each miner then organised whatever assistance he needed to transport the coal from where he cut it to where it was needed, wherever possible using members of his immediate or extended family.

The practices of the cottage economy where families worked together as economic units, contributing effort according to their individual ability, transferred to the mining industry. It was not an effective transfer. Long hours, unnatural postures and inability to take breaks pushed the bodies of workers to the limits they were capable of enduring. As pits attempted to exploit seams further away from the entrance assistants had to move the coal longer distances and a miner may have needed more than one helper. Some married women seem to have abandoned underground work as soon as enough children of either sex were strong enough to assist their father. In mines that had low passages and restricted space children were smaller and more flexible and could drag coal tubs much more easily than an adult woman who found the passages a tight fit.

In some medium-sized pits rails were laid, at least along main roadways. This reduced the need to drag tubs for long distances along rough or muddy floors. Once the tubs were hauled to a railed section of the mine they could be pushed. Older miners reported that this made the work faster. Workers did not benefit when rails were installed because tubs often became heavier. The size of a coal container was determined by the dimensions of the passage, not the weight that a hurrier could realistically move. Adult women again began to be displaced by strong lads or a couple of children whose combined strength exceeded that of the woman. The female workforce started to edge towards one that was predominantly made up of children and unmarried women.

Although a female's work became easier in pits where rails were installed, coal bearing in Scotland became more much more difficult. It was always a dreadful task but early mines were not deep, which meant that loads did not have to be carried too far. This allowed bearers to make more journeys carrying lesser weights. Elizabeth Paterson, a seventy-year-old bearer, recollected that when she was was young she had never needed to stay underground longer than it took for one candle to burn itself out.

As mines became deeper women responded to the longer distances required of them by increasing the amount of coal they carried on each journey to keep their working time to a minimum. Some miners needed two assistants to move their coal and young girls were often found working alongside their mothers. Increased weight may have caused adult coal bearers to develop more health problems than experienced by previous generations as heavier loads bore down on their bodies for longer. It is possible that the early nineteenth century witnessed coal bearing move from an occupation which was arduous and unpleasant to one that destroyed female health.

Wales was similar to Scotland in that some of its seams were closer to vertical than horizontal. Unlike Scotland coal from these seams was raised to the surface by winding gear known as a windlass. Women wound the coal up through the mine rather than carrying it on their backs. Windlass work was not well-paid relative to the effort that it required but it did mean that women's bodies were not being broken by the repeated carrying of loads that were too heavy. As the winding gear needed the strength of a woman or an older adolescent this method also prevented the employment of young girls in a dangerous activity that was beyond their strength.

Children of both sexes entered the workplace at a young age. Sometimes there was a financial advantage as local customs had developed in some places to ensure that a man earned enough money to support his family. The amount of coal a miner was allowed to cut might depend on the number of assistants he had underground with him. Even when a child was not strong enough to provide effort the payment could be claimed if other family members did the work so long as the child was physically present in the mine.

Welsh boys were carried underground almost as soon as they could stand so that their father could claim an allowance for them. Girls did not have monetary value and were taken underground when they were considered able to assist. At Cumgwrach, Neath, in June 1820, six-year-old Elizabeth Pendry and twelve-year-old Annie Tonks died in an explosion. Elizabeth may have been the youngest girl to die underground.

In pits that did not use this system of payment there were other reasons for taking young children underground. Sometimes the child could perform a limited amount of easy work until it fell asleep or a small play area might have been created where the child could amuse itself whilst its parents worked. James Waugh, a sixty-year-old Scottish miner, took his 'bairns' down early to keep them out of mischief. He spoke of a daughter who had been underground for eight years but only working for five. For the first three she did little below ground but play. Children could be safer underground than they were above it. The commission report is littered with details of unnamed children who died or were seriously injured from inadequate childcare.

Women who offered their services looking after children were often not suitable for the task because they were too old or disabled. Unable to perform any other job, they were paid by working mothers to look after young children, sometimes charging most of the money the woman earned. Some took young babies and toddlers into their own beds. They dipped knotted rags in opiates and used as them as dummies to quieten fractious babies. Children who could walk were left to run around outside without supervision or, if necessary, discipline. Whether the child received anything to eat was a matter of chance.

If it was at all possible mothers tried to avoid paying for childcare. Younger members of the family were left at home with an older sister who was a child herself and too immature to be responsible for keeping little ones safe or maintaining control over mischievous toddlers. In 1841 Mary Glover had no qualms about leaving three young children in the care of their twelve-year-old sister, a wench who had a palsy. Alison Adam's siblings aged four and seven were locked in the house whilst their mother and older sister were at work. Occasionally a neighbour looked in to check them.

Several doctors remarked on the deaths of young children in accidents that had arisen from them being left in the care of a child who was far too young for the responsibility. Toddlers burned to death through their clothes catching fire or fatally scalded themselves by upsetting pots of boiling liquid. Babies were dropped and sustained fractured skulls. One of the advantages of married women leaving mining and looking after the home was an improved level of care for young children.

The key determinant of the amount of work a female miner had to do was the state of the economy. When demand was buoyant and coal prices were high a collier could earn a good wage without too much effort. When the market for coal collapsed and wages tumbled miners increased their hours in order to maintain their income. If food became expensive they would try to produce additional coal so that they did not have to reduce their personal consumption.

A woman had to move the amount of coal her husband or father had contracted to produce. When times were bad she had to do more work. When they were good she could find herself working hard but irregularly if the miner took a few days off and then had to put in long shifts to hew the amount agreed by the next pay day.

Only a few miners had any interest in working to better themselves. Most knew how much money they needed to maintain the lifestyle they desired and adjusted their hours of work to achieve this. Their life expectancy was between forty to fifty years, a product of the harsh nature of work, which rendered many of them old men at a time when other workers were in their prime. Miners Thomas Gibson and George Bryan told the 1833 Factory Commission that by the age of fifteen rheumatism could be a serious problem for workers in wet pits. In later years respiratory complaints and skeletal disorders often developed. Any worker who survived beyond fifty tended either to live off parish relief or the coal master found him a task which he could still perform.

✳   ✳   ✳

Miners knew that they risked their lives every time they went to work. Many treated each day as if it was their last, drinking and indulging in exuberant leisure activities such as dog and cock fighting. They returned to the pit only when they needed to replenish their money.

Working underground had always been dangerous but as pits became deeper the risks increased and accidents became more frequent and more serious. Owners and workers were almost equally culpable. Owners had an ill-defined and unenforceable duty to protect the safety of the workers they employed. Some made little effort to ensure safety, others made none at all. Any safety technique or equipment introduced into the mine was regarded as a method of enabling dangerous work to be undertaken, not a way of protecting human life. A Staffordshire mine that constructed brick domes above some disused shafts discovered that they had been broken down and the bricks taken away by miners for their own use.

Workers also colluded in unsafe practices underground. They routinely ignored safety procedures, usually so that they could work more quickly and get out of the mine as soon as possible. Inquest reports for these decades contain examples of negligence or contributory negligence on the part of workers.

In an underground visit in 1841, sub-Commissioner Scriven described how he found himself surrounded by gas in Wyke Lane pit and knocked the safety lamp out of the hand of the collier lad who was acting as his guide to stop him trying to blow the flame through its protecting gauze shield. Had the boy succeeded the result could have been a fatal explosion. Scriven and the boy then had to feel their way back through the passages to the mine shaft, hoping not to be hit by a corve rolling along at great speed and unable to see them in the dark. Sub-Commissioner Symons refused to descend a mine shaft in Barnsley, concerned for his own safety, after observing the worn condition of the rope hauling the pit cage.

Underground explosions were the hazards that resulted in the greatest loss of life. They were caused by gas igniting. A variety of gases occur naturally in rocks and can seep out and build up in quantity. Not all the gases found underground are harmful to health but an explosion can cause them to combine to form something toxic. The common gases found underground became known as 'damps'. The term comes from the German word *dampf*, which means vapour. It was brought to Britain by immigrant workers from Holland who developed some early mines.

Methane gas was known as firedamp. Carbon monoxide was called whitedamp. The mixture of gases that form in the aftermath of an explosion in a confined space was variously known as afterdamp, black-damp, chokedamp or stythe. The components of this toxic aftermath include carbon dioxide, carbon monoxide, water and nitrogen. The damps were completed by hydrogen sulphide with its distinctive odour of rotten eggs, appropriately known as stinkdamp.

Methane gas can escape when the rock is disturbed. There are critical concentrations at which it explodes into a fireball if it comes into contact with a source of ignition. The candles used by miners were capable of igniting an explosion. Early in the century Humphrey Davy and George Stephenson each invented a miner's safety lamp which protected the candle frame, reducing the possibility of sparking an explosion. Miners disliked the lamps because the protective gauze reduced the amount of light available and they often deliberately damaged the gauze, negating the protection afforded by the lamp.

As an explosion of methane gives out tremendous heat, burns were a serious hazard. The gaseous by-products of the explosion varied depending upon the chemicals that were in the atmosphere. Whitedamp and afterdamp formed rapidly displacing oxygen from the air. Anyone unable to escape from an explosion in a confined area could die very quickly from suffocation as oxygen was used up. In small explosions those affected were often dragged out unconscious but alive by colleagues.

A final hazard resulting from even a small explosion of methane was that it could ignite coal dust in the area and produce a much larger explosion.

Methane could be present for a variety of reasons. Breaking into a new wall of coal either with gunpowder or with tools could release a large, unexpected pocket of gas. In mines that were not adequately ventilated a small, unnoticed seepage of gas could build up in a tunnel to an explosive concentration. As mining moved into deeper seams explosions which resulted in heavy loss of life became more frequent. The number of females who featured in accident or inquest reports is low in comparison with men and boys. It indicates that the number of females who worked underground at this time was not large.

At the William pit in Whitehaven in October 1823 two unnamed girls died in an explosion of firedamp, whilst in 1826 an unnamed woman suffocated at a mine in Worsley. In 1806 Mary Rylance died in a fire at St Helens alongside her young son; and in May 1831 fourteen-year-old Mary Cunliffe perished at Haydock with other members of her family in an explosion.

Another major cause of underground accidents was falling roofs or debris. Sometime this was the result of inadequate propping of tunnels. On other occasions the roof was formed from a soft and crumbly material immediately above the coal seam. Added to this were risks to workers' lives from breaking ropes and chains as either they or their trucks were being lowered or raised and falls into the pit from ground level when they strayed too close to holes which were not properly fenced off. With such a high level of danger constantly around them it is not surprising that many miners opted to live solely for the present.

Flooding was also an ever-present hazard. The earth's natural movement, or excavation by miners, could create create gaps for water to seep or break through. Exceptional and sudden rainfall could also cause inundations, especially in the relatively shallow drift mines. In July 1838, a freak storm caused the deaths of three men in Rochdale and twenty-six children at Silkstone near Barnsley (see Chapter 2) when flash floods cascaded into the underground workings.

✳   ✳   ✳

A few workers saved money. They were enterprising men who were trying to better themselves by becoming pit owners. Landowners often granted mining rights in exchange for a royalty per ton of coal extracted, especially in areas where seams were thin. Numerous small pits opened up on both sides of the Pennines, paid for by men who worked hard and managed to save enough money to finance the sinking of a shaft.

It is likely that several members of a family contributed towards accumulating the capital as the investment ensured that family members had a way of earning a living. At the Meal Hill pit in Yorkshire Rachel Tinker was a distant cousin of owner Uriah Tinker. Her father worked as the banksman. Scottish miner Alison Adam is believed to have been a relative of a pit overseer. Alison and her mother may have been given their jobs after her father died. Claims of kinship went no further than the provision of a job. Rachel worked under the same bad conditions as the rest of the youngsters in the pit and did the same job.

Coal from small pits did not make much income for the lessee. Ebenezer Healey, who worked alongside Rachel Tinker in 1841, owned a mine in the same locality towards the end of the century. The census shows that his daughters worked as weavers, suggesting that the income from operating a small mine would not keep a large family.

✳   ✳   ✳

In the early nineteenth century very little was known about mining families. Their working hours were spent out of the sight of casual observers and it was assumed that they lived as a segregated caste in separate communities, marrying amongst themselves and unfit company for the rest of society. Some outsiders may even have believed that mining families lived as well as worked underground.

During the late eighteenth and early nineteenth centuries a few writers travelled around the country recording their impressions of the places they visited. Had segregated, unruly communities of miners existed it is likely that at least one would have been discovered. William Cobbett encountered miners when travelling in the north east of England and described the people he met in the same terms as other types of worker.

The 1841 census and the evidence of witnesses to the commission indicate that the notion that miners lived separately was incorrect. Even when mining took place a few miles beyond industrial heartlands or in less populated rural locations there were usually weavers' or farm workers' cottages in the vicinity.

In 1841 pit owner Thomas Wilson of Silkstone, near Barnsley, tetchily suggested that it would be impossible to make owners responsible for educating mining children because local mining families were intermingled with nail makers and agricultural labourers and providing separate schools was impractical. Around Bury, miners, agricultural workers and cottage weavers lived in close proximity. In populous areas such as Elland near Huddersfield the neighbours of a miner were more likely to be mill workers and weavers rather than other miners. The Commission report indicated that by 1841 the village of Worsborough in Barnsley was inhabited by a large number of mining families. This was true but the census reveals that there were linen weavers, bleachers, glass-blowers and shoemakers living alongside them. The Scottish and Welsh censuses reveal similar patterns with sufficient intermingling of occupations to indicate that communities were mixed rather than discrete occupational groups.

The myth that miners lived separately may have arisen because outside observers expected them to have dirty, dust-blackened hands and faces. As miners usually washed when they returned home from the pit they would have looked no different to anyone else except when walking home from work. Sub-Commissioner Wood suggested that miners conformed to the same social norms as those who lived around them. Those living in neighbourhoods where there was a greater proportion of middle-class residents sometimes adopted middle-class values. Their posture might have become a little deformed and they might walk with a shuffling gait but unless a miner or mining lass conspicuously drew attention to their occupation, it is likely that no-one would realise what it was.

The extent of intermarriage between mining families and those carrying out different occupations is unclear but miners married mill workers, servants, farmers' daughters and dressmakers. No evidence of mining girls marrying anyone other than a miner has been identified. It was reported that mining girls were deficient in domestic skills and not sought out by men who followed other occupations. An alternative explanation is that there were only a handful of marriageable mining girls available at any time and a large number of miners. Girls had a good chance of finding a partner from within the circle of men they met at work and did not have to look more widely.

Some witnesses to the Commission considered that miners, both men and women, could be distinguished from other workers by the amount of alcohol they consumed. In liking beer and whisky they were little different from other workers but the higher wages earned by miners enabled them to buy more and display the effects of intoxication more visibly. Miners had a very practical reason for drinking heavily. Like workers in a number of factories they worked in hot, dry, dusty conditions. They sweated profusely and breathed in dust. A long drink of beer helped to slake their thirst and to replace fluid in the system. In the early part of the nineteenth century beer was often brewed in the home. It was regarded as a temperance beverage and once brewed, could be stored and drunk without the need for any further preparation.

At this time water was not a practical source of hydration. It was not available on tap in the home and had to be drawn from the nearest pump or stream and then boiled to purify it. This meant using fuel, which had to be paid for. When boiled, water, or the tea or coffee made with it, had to cool down before it could be swallowed.

The criticism of workers of all types for heavy drinking was an unfortunate one. Although it is likely that many regarded the temporary sense of well-being that came from intoxication as a welcome escape from the pain and drudgery of the working day they needed to replace fluids that had been lost in a very hot working environment. There was not a safe way to do this. Beer could lead to drunken behaviour, which offended the middle-classes, but contaminated water had potentially adverse side effects which could affect a worker's ability to go out and earn a living.

At the beginning of the century the conditions endured by workers were of little interest to many of the owners who were being made rich from the products of their labour. The first two decades saw a period of savage repression of workers by a succession of governments. After the horrors of the French Revolution, the ruling classes worried that British workers might also rise in revolt and brought in a number of measures designed to prevent this. By the 1820s the reign of terror was slipping out of living memory, a sense of proportion was restored and some of the repressive measures were lightened. One of these happened in 1824 when the Combination Acts were repealed.

The aim of the Combination Acts had been to prevent working men acting together for political purposes. They were allowed to join together for social purposes, and some provident societies to which workers subscribed a few pence of their weekly wages as social insurance against being unable to work through illness or accident dated from this time. The number of societies increased after 1824 and many miners paid into at least one fund, often linked to the pit at which they worked, in order to provide for themselves and their dependants in times of adversity. Owners of large and medium-sized pits sometimes contributed to the funds collected by the men, particularly if a worker was killed or seriously injured at work.

Some societies began to develop a political emphasis, identifying to members the perceived benefits of acting as a group and sometimes advocating approaches designed to secure higher wages. It was not organised union activity but a new dynamic was developing amongst miners, that of loyalty to a group of co-workers and consideration of what was best for the group rather than what was best for the individual and his family.

❊   ❊   ❊

The generation of women who lived and worked in mining families in the first three decades of the nineteenth century experienced many changes in their lives at work and at home. Whether change benefited them or made their work harder depended on where they lived and their position in the family. Although the work of children, unmarried girls and coal bearers probably became more difficult some married women were able to leave the workforce. Those who who lived in places where the coal was good quality and mines had been improved could benefit from the security provided by a man in regular employment who contributed to a friendly society. These women were able to leave work permanently and concentrate on running a home.

Around 1830 Britain entered a period of rapid social, technological and political progress. The changes experienced by the mining women up to this time were slight in comparison to the ones that would transform their lives in the next twenty years.

CHAPTER 2

The Winds of Change
How mining developed in the 1830s

I know the corves are very heavy. They are the biggest corves anywhere about. The work is far too hard for me. The sweat runs off me all over sometimes.

Ann Eggley, 18, hurrier

The 1830s was a decade of significant modernisation. Developments within the coal mining industry and outside it changed the role of female workers and affected attitudes towards them. The extent and implications were not fully understood at the time. By the end of the decade females were leaving underground work at a faster rate than they were being replaced. It is impossible to put a figure on this but with several large employers preventing women working in their pits the composition of the workforce was becoming predominantly male. The change was driven by business considerations, though removing females from the drudgery of mine work and giving them the opportunity to look after their families would have appealed to the social conscience of some of the more philanthropic owners.

Whenever deeper seams were opened owners incurred substantial costs in sinking shafts and quarrying underground roadways. Needing to secure a reasonable return on their investment, they began to pay greater attention to the economics of bringing coal to the surface. They identified that it was more cost effective to invest in good conditions for moving coal underground and increase the size of trucks rather than employ large numbers of workers to move small loads. This meant that fewer workers were needed but they had to be strong enough to fill and move heavy trucks. In Scotland the Duke of Buccleugh and Mr Ramsey of Rosewell Barleydene excluded all females from their pits around 1837. James Wright, the duke's pit steward, explained that where mines were well railed and properly maintained strong lads could accomplish singly much more work than masses of female children. John Wright, who worked for Mr Ramsey, found that men were prepared to attend more regularly when the working conditions were improved, which boosted output.

The role of a woman as a homemaker was important to employers and to some workers who believed that having a woman at home able to concentrate on domestic tasks enabled a man to be more healthy, which meant that he could attend work more regularly and be more productive when he was there. In the Scottish mines where women were excluded it was noted that within a few years the health and moral condition of whole families improved. Whether this was entirely the result of women remaining at home is debatable. Men were not prepared to tolerate the damp, cramped passages which women had been expected to work in. It is likely that improvements to working conditions and not having to carry heavy loads on their backs contributed much towards the increase in well-being amongst mining families.

Earl Fitzwilliam's pits near Barnsley had employed men as hurriers and also used ponies in the main passages for some years. In Manchester the Bridgewater Estate stopped all married women and girls under twelve from working in their mines. Some managers phased out female labour more subtly, permitting those already employed to remain in work but not taking on any further women.

In mines of all sizes and in many different areas boys became a more acceptable choice than females as assistants. Female miners worked underground in Cumberland in the early part of the nineteenth century but when the Royal Commission visited in 1841, only one very old mine still employed women.

Some owners instructed their stewards that females should not be allowed underground when the practice began to arouse public disgust. At Gomersall, Mr Harrison permitted two girls to work as a favour to a needy family. Brookes and Greaves of Dewsbury only allowed girls to work for their father. Some pits that allowed girls to work dismissed them at fourteen, considering this to be the age at which it became unacceptable for them to be working with members of the opposite sex.

Workers who wanted to take a wife or daughter underground faced the choice of working in their preferred pit and bringing a boy to help them or moving to a different pit where a female might be allowed. It was a risky strategy for owners and only likely to have been successful in preventing female labour where there were no alternative employers or everyone in the district applied the same rule.

✳   ✳   ✳

The employment of females underground began to be seen by some miners as something to be avoided if possible, even if the local pit allowed female labour. John Oldham from Lancashire and Joseph Fraser from Scotland refused to allow their wives to continue to work underground to protect the woman's welfare. In Barnsley and parts of west Yorkshire, it was becoming normal for female miners to stop working when they married. The same convention developed in Alloa and parts of Fife.

In some areas other industries developed alongside mining and families chose for women to work in factories rather than at a colliery. Women in East Manchester flocked to the cotton mills. In parts of west Yorkshire where the woollen industry was expanding a similar change was taking place. Very few females from Leeds and Bradford worked underground and the ones who did tended to be too young to work in factories.

✳   ✳   ✳

The age at which girls were taken to the pit was increasing. Around 1810, Jane Wood and Mary Glover began to work when they were seven and Mary Ann Watson at five. Ann Eggley started work at seven in 1830 though Elizabeth Day and Sarah Jowett who were of similar age had begun at eight and nine. By 1841 a number of girls under fifteen reported that they had started working when they were nine or ten or occasionally older. Whilst the ability of younger girls to move big trucks was a factor, repugnance was developing amongst miners about young girls working underground. Some miners seem to have made determined efforts to keep their daughters away from the pits or, if it was unavoidable, to delay the start as long as they could. Samuel Well described girls working underground as unnatural, indecent and uncalled for. Rather than taking their children out to work in age order some miners may have taken younger sons in preference and only used girls as a last resort.

The fact that some miners refused to allow their daughters to work underground created the opportunity for young girls from non-mining families to work in the industry, at least until they were old enough to take a job in a mill. In Yorkshire, the 1830s saw the collapse of hand-loom weaving as a viable means of providing for a family. Cottage weavers who had no prospect of maintaining an adequate standard of living on their meagre earnings clung to their dying craft with surprising tenacity for many years, hoping for the industry to revive. Refusing to take work in a factory or follow an alternative trade themselves they hired their young sons and daughters to miners who did not have children of their own. Daughters of agricultural workers also found themselves working in mines to stave off family starvation.

An entirely different factor, and one that contributed to women in some areas leaving pit work, was the development of collective thinking amongst male workers about women's and men's roles in the workplace and whether some industries should be for men only. In Bathgate, the men were reported to have a strong objection to women labouring underground, not from the soreness of the work but from a notion that it would cheapen their labour. At one point the men agreed amongst themselves that their wives would not work. The voluntary agreement eventually broke down in the face of labour shortages.

For miners who were prepared to keep their womenfolk out of the pits it was a short step to believing that all women should stay away. According to Lanarkshire overseer Thomas Stevenson, many men who kept their wives at home objected to the conduct of others who continued the bad practice.

Even when there was no formal organisation, men had ample opportunity to exchange views in beer houses and underground. Workers gave no hint of being involved in collective activity to the sub-Commissioners but several owners and managers referred to it. William Wilson of Denny explained that men held secret conclaves in the mines and that his business often felt the effects of private combination.

It is unlikely that a meeting of 350 working colliers from the Barnsley area could have been convened, apparently at short notice on the initiative of the colliers, when the sub-Commissioner was in the town without rudimentary networks and co-ordination. There are no indications that female workers were present at the meeting. The miners discussed and passed six resolutions on a show of hands. Improving wages and increasing employment opportunities for men and teenage boys underpinned them. One resolution stated that the employment of females in mining was not proper work for females and that it was a scandalous practice. Only five dissented and those supporting it included miners whose daughters were working underground.

The odium that was reported in some areas about women working in pits owed more to a belief that the industry would provide a better living for men if women were not allowed to work in it than to the fact that the work was too hard for a lass. Earl Fitzwilliam's mines did not employ women and paid higher wages to men. Scottish owners who excluded women indicated that the improvements they had made to their pits enabled a man with a couple of lads to earn as much as the entire family had done previously.

A miner's perception that the employment of women led to lower wages and poorer working conditions had some validity. Improved underground infrastructure, exclusion of females, higher productivity and increased earnings were linked together. Working conditions, rather than the gender of the workers, were the key factor in increasing output. Productivity would have improved with women moving coal in good working conditions but the increase was unlikely to have been as great as that realised by the greater strength of males.

Collective action was overt in the East Manchester area. Miners deliberately tightened the labour supply in 1830 and secured a short-lived increase in wages. They were very sensitive to any potential encroachment of women into what was regarded as a male industry. This may have stemmed from experience of local cotton factories employing women in preference to men because they could pay less for the work. Two incidents demonstrate the collective refusal of men to accept women working at mines and the willingness of owners to sanction this.

One woman worked at Greaves's Pit for a week but the men said they would leave if she continued and so both she and her husband were forced to go. The couple were given 14 shillings from a miners' provident fund to compensate them. A man from Wigan went to work in Oldham but decided to leave when he discovered that his wife was not allowed to work alongside him in the pit.

Staffordshire was another area where the role of women was being questioned by men. Women did not work underground but approximately 1,000 were employed in surface occupations in 1841. Sub-Commissioner Mitchell reported that some men objected to girls being employed outdoors in what was considered to be laborious work. He concluded that as men had already claimed some forms of work for themselves caution should be exercised in further restricting the ways in which women could earn their living.

During the 1830s, miners throughout the country were becoming receptive to the idea that mining ought to be a male preserve. In places where mining communities were developing the collective view of neighbours and colleagues may have influenced the attitude of individual workers about whether their wives or daughters worked underground. As long as family income did not fall below what was needed to live on it is likely that most women regarded a husband's or father's decision that they should stop working as welcome news.

✳   ✳   ✳

Alongside the changes that were taking place within coal mining a number of political and social developments gathered momentum in the 1830s, influencing the way in which people who were not involved began to view the industry.

In the eighteenth century, factory industry developed on the economic principle known as *laissez faire*. This deemed that the wages and conditions agreed between a worker and his employer were freely negotiated by both parties taking account of the state of the market and the wage a worker needed to enable him to live. There was no acknowledgement of any inequality of bargaining position on the part of a worker whose alternative to long hours, low wages and bad conditions was homelessness and starvation.

Government and Parliament tended to remain aloof from legislative interference in how industries were run. Many members of the House of Lords owned vast estates whose agricultural and mineral wealth they exploited ruthlessly. Members of the House of Commons were often relatives or placemen of noble families, local gentry or self-made men who had secured social respectability through money made by trade or commerce. Both Houses had vested interests in maintaining that economic endeavour should take place independently of any regulation unless regulation assisted the employer. Any interference by Parliament on matters relating to how a man earned his crust or made his fortune was vigorously opposed as being wrong in principle and liable to provoke economic disaster.

Parliament had only once intervened decisively in matters of commerce when in 1807 it had abolished the slave trade. Otherwise, despite occasional rhetoric, it remained aloof from action that might impinge on the free operation of the market. The Chimney Sweeps Act of 1788, which regulated the use of climbing boys, stood out as unusual interference. A Factories Act, designed to regulate conditions for apprentices, was passed in 1802 but proved ineffective. Another law passed in 1819 was equally toothless and widely ignored. The common feature of all three acts was that they protected the interests of groups of workers who were in an unequal bargaining position with their employers. The flaw was that there was no means of enforcing their provisions.

The first decisive sign of changing attitudes about the role of Parliament and the influence of public opinion came in 1832, when after three years of increasing public agitation, reform of the House of Commons took place. Wealthy businessmen and entrepreneurs had been vocal in calls for change to make the House of Commons relevant to an industrial society.

The reforms abolished some rural constituencies where population movement meant that there were no longer many voters and gave seats instead to some newly industrialised towns, which until that point had no representation. The right to vote was extended but as voters needed to own property of a specified value those who benefited were employers rather than workers.

The reformed House of Commons was no more sympathetic to the conditions of workers than its predecessor had been. Members were still drawn from the traditional ruling class or were men who had prospered through trade and been assimilated into society. Many of them believed implicitly in the principles of *laissez faire* and the rights of employers. What the reform demonstrated was that the opinions of the middle-classes could be a successful catalyst for change.

Whilst the reform of the House of Commons was taking place, co-ordinated calls for changes in the working practices in factories were gathering momentum in the country and in Parliament. The impetus was moral and humanitarian with small numbers of influential people, some of them factory owners, speaking out against the hours that factory workers were forced to work, the inhumane punishments inflicted on those who fell asleep or made mistakes and the injuries and deaths caused by unsafe machines and working practices. The remedy that these campaigners advocated was a limitation of the working day in factories to ten hours. It was unlikely that Parliament would legislate so decisively but, based on the few earlier precedents, it was possible that improvements could be obtained for children. This was expected to reduce the hours that adults would be able to work.

Parliament was loosely divided into two groups, the Tories tended to represent the traditional landed interest and the Whigs would represent enterprise and industry. The ten hours campaigners drew support from members of both groups though Tories tended to be more supportive than Whigs as change would not affect their own financial interest. As social matters were not considered to be the business of government MPs were free to follow their beliefs or consciences about improving workers' conditions.

In 1832, Michael Sadler, a supporter of factory reform, introduced a bill to limit the working hours of children in factories. Many believed that he was exaggerating the abuses he described and Parliament set up a select committee, under Sadler's chairmanship, to ascertain the facts. The evidence it garnered was damning of industrial practices but before any legislation could be passed to address this Sadler ceased to be an MP. His seat was one of those that had been abolished and although he stood in a new constituency his opponent was elected.

The Ten Hours campaigners urgently needed a new leader. Their choice was Lord Anthony Ashley Cooper, MP for Dorset and son and heir of the sixth Earl of Shaftesbury. His family background was Tory but he had personal links with several Whigs. Lord Ashley already had a record of bringing about social change. In 1828 he secured a change in the law to improve the care afforded to people with severe mental health problems. His reforming zeal was driven by his strong Christian conscience and he believed passionately in the need to improve the lives of the poor and marginalised. He interpreted this in terms of improving their immediate living and working conditions, not in change to the established political order, and had been a prominent opponent of reforming the House of Commons.

Ashley agreed to re-introduce Sadler's bill but met with strong opposition. Sadler's report was too horrific to be ignored, but many owners believed that he deliberately sought out isolated and extreme examples and had failed to produce a fair and balanced picture of the textile industry. The Whig party now formed the government and decided to tackle the raging controversy by asking the king to appoint a Royal Commission to inquire into the work of children in textile factories. A steer was given to the Commissioners that the report should correct the unfavourable evidence highlighted by Sadler and produce a more balanced and benign view of textile manufacturing.

The remit given to the commission had tacitly conceded that change would follow when it referred to identifying the propriety and means of curtailing children's hours of labour to enable Parliament to legislate on the subject. The Commission's report, which was published in 1833, confirmed that Sadler had exaggerated but concluded that bad practices were ingrained in factories and children should be afforded protection.

The government decided to lead the process of passing new laws. Lord Althorp, the Leader of the House of Commons, quickly championed a bill to deal with the worst problems. No child under nine was to work and those under thirteen were restricted to not more than eight hours. Employers had to be satisfied of a child's age before allowing him to work and to provide two hours of education each day. Four factory inspectors were appointed to check that the law was being obeyed, the first time that any powers of enforcement had been included in legislation.

The Factory Act fell well short of the objective of achieving the ten hours working day and Ashley, supported by fellow MP and mill owner John Fielden, refused to let the issue disappear from view using any new information about the conditions of workers to reopen the discussion. Supporters sent letters to the press about factory conditions. Even though the campaign made no practical progress those who opposed any further reform were never able to conclude that the factory question had been dealt with decisively. Those who were open-minded on the subject were regularly made aware that there was much about industrial working conditions they knew nothing about.

Not only had the factory enquiries discovered abuses that had needed to be remedied, the annual reports produced by the new factory inspectors continued to reveal a woeful picture of working conditions and employers who acted in defiance of the law.

In 1833, as part of his investigation of Lancashire's mills, Assistant Commissioner Edward Tufnell had paid a brief visit to a mine in Worsley. He interviewed three miners, visited two pits and discovered that children worked in holes which were too small for adults. He concluded that the hardest labour in the worst room in the worst-conducted factory was less hard and less demoralising than the labour in the best of coal mines. In the charged atmosphere surrounding the textile factory investigation this passed with little comment at the time.

Descriptions of miners working in seams as hot as ovens, or in wet pits with water running from the roof into their eyes, sometimes unable to eat because of dust, damp and foulness of the air, refluxing food as a result of being bent double, old women suffocating to death underground and children working in low, narrow seams were all ugly images, which once enshrined in an official report could not remain hidden away from wider notice.

An uneasy awareness that large numbers of children worked underground without anyone knowing what they did spread across the country towards the end of the decade as a result of newspaper reports. When easily accessible seams of coal became exhausted, owners tunnelled deeper. Small and medium-sized pits often tried to do this in the cheapest way possible, took risks and did little to prevent unsafe methods of working. Underground accidents were frequent and the number of casualties grew.

Regional newspapers in the late 1830s regularly recorded the unpleasant manner of death of women and girls. At Blackrod in October 1836 Alice Anderton, Margaret Anderton, Sarah Grayson, Ellin Sherrington and Catherine Wilson died from severe burns after a firedamp explosion. It was caused by the fireman walking into the pit with a lighted tar rope. In the national press the accident received a mention but gave no names. When a worker was shown to have caused the accident owners could shrug their shoulders and deny any culpability.

Margaret Davies and Jane Legg died in an explosion at Nantyglo in Monmouthshire in December 1837. At Blaenavon in November 1838 Mary Hale and Elizabeth Harwood were drowned when the mine flooded. In 1839 Ann Jenkins fell down a pit shaft at the Graig Colliery. Sarah Bevan was killed by falling coal at a pit at Merthyr.

In 1840, three women working for the Bridgewater Trust lost their lives. Isabella Holme and Betty Turner were killed when they were thrown out of the bucket in which they were descending the pit shaft and Margaret Evans lingered a painful fortnight after being severely burned by firedamp.

Accidents that were not fatal were no less unpleasant. By the time she was sixteen Helen Reid had had two close brushes with death. In 1839 she was trapped underground for two days at the Edmondstone colliery with twelve other people when the roof collapsed. The group survived for two days without food or light and at one point were up to their chins in water. Eventually they struggled through the workings to an old shaft from which they were rescued. Early in 1841 she was filling tubs when faulty equipment latched onto her clothes and carried her up the shaft. Helen was lucky. Her hand clasped tightly onto the chain and she fainted with fright as she was dragged upwards. Helen Bowman of Donnybristle was not so fortunate. The basket hooks that caught her pit clothes dragged her almost to the top of the shaft before she fell. She died two days later, a few days before she was to have been married.

The most tragic of all accidents in this period was the disaster that unfolded in a Yorkshire village on the afternoon of Wednesday, 4 July 1838. The day was hot and dry until the early afternoon when a freak storm of extreme ferocity hit both sides of the Pennines. Contemporary newspapers reported torrents of rain, hailstones of up to 4 inches in circumference and flash floods that tore up hedges and trees, swept away cattle and lifted railway sleepers. The hailstones broke nearly all the panes of the glass house at Wentworth Castle causing about £500 of damage and were not fully melted by the following morning.

At the Huskar Pit in Silkstone water started seeping into the engine house and the banksman signalled to the workers below to evacuate the pit. As the workers congregated at the shaft waiting for the pit cage to descend the engine powering the cage lost steam. As it stopped working panic broke out amongst the children and teenagers. Against the advice of the experienced miners forty youngsters set off up a passage intending to walk out of the pit through a day hole entrance. A few yards inside the day hole's mouth they scrambled through a ventilation door to the outside. As they did so an adjacent stream, swollen with the afternoon's deluge, suddenly overflowed and cascaded towards them. The force of the water swept the young escapers back into the passage, knocking them off their feet. Moments later eleven girls and fifteen boys aged between seven and seventeen lay drowned in a passage twelve yards long. The water, which flooded into the passage, had been no more than 6 inches deep according to the marks on the wall but with nowhere to escape to it rose up against the ventilation door.

The deaths of Elizabeth Carr, Elizabeth Clarkson, Catherine Garnett, Elizabeth Hollins, Sarah Jukes, Ann Moss, Sarah Newton, Ellen Parker, Mary Sellars, Hannah Taylor and Hannah Webster shocked the country. A report in *The Times* named the victims rather than just referring to yet another pit accident. This was an unusual amount of detail and it brought to the attention of surprised readers that girls worked underground. The tragedy also came to the notice of Queen Victoria, herself only a few years older than seventeen-year-old Hannah Taylor, the oldest of the victims.

In May 1841, Matilda Carr, Hannah Clarkson and Ann Hollins gave evidence to the Children's Employment Commission. None referred to the accident probably reflecting that sibling death was not unusual. The effect on the Carr family can perhaps be seen in Matilda's evidence. She had worked for just one week as her father could no longer keep the family without her help. Eleven was old to start hurrying and it may be that her parents tried to avoid sending another daughter underground. They had also called their new baby daughter Elizabeth after her dead sister.

Huskar was an unusual accident. Nineteenth-century inquests into mining deaths usually returned verdicts of accidental death despite hearing evidence that a modern perspective sees as causal culpability on the part of a worker or manager. For the children of Huskar there is no other conclusion but that the deaths were accidental, the result of a freak, unforeseeable set of circumstances. The news made very uncomfortable reading for anyone with a conscience about the conditions children worked in or the age at which they had to go out to get a living.

✻   ✻   ✻

As the 1830s drew to a close, two causes began to dominate politics and newspaper coverage to the exclusion of almost anything else. One of these was Chartism, a working-class movement aspiring to improve the conditions of working men. The Chartists were a very diverse group of campaigners who saw political change as the key to improving conditions, rather than social or employment reform. As Parliament had already bowed to public pressure and reformed itself Chartist leaders put their energies into campaigning for all men to be allowed to vote in elections, annual elections, payment of MPs and secret ballots. Their lack of emphasis on social reforms may have weakened the influence of middle-class reformers as such changes were not ones that workers were placing high in their list of priorities.

Whilst workers were pre-occupied with Chartism the important issue for industrialists was free trade. Manufacturers considered that Britain's prosperity depended on free trading between nations with no artificial barriers being in place to distort the market and keep prices unnecessarily high. The most potent of all tariffs were the Corn Laws which had been passed in 1815 to protect British landowners from being undercut by imported foreign wheat. Manufacturers believed that they were subsidising agriculturalists as the wages paid to workers were in part determined by what workers had to pay for food. Manufacturers argued that repealing the Corn Laws would enable cheaper grain to be imported and this would reduce the price of bread. Cheaper bread would allow factory wages to fall as workers would be able to buy their food at a lower price. Countries that exported grain to Britain would receive currency, which they would spend on products from British manufacturers, maintaining or increasing employment. It was a virtuous circle which that maximise the country's prosperity. The loser would be domestic agriculture which was obtaining a significant wealth from the fact that the price of grain was kept artificially high.

The debate had some links to calls for further factory reform with manufacturers pointing out that workers' lives could be improved by repealing the Corn Laws as they would then be able to reduce their hours of work. Repeal would mean that landowners would face a loss of income. If workers' lives were improved by reducing the length of the working day the costs would fall on factory owners.

By summer 1840 the Whig government was limping towards the end of its years in office. With the Corn Law debate heightening tensions between the manufacturing and agricultural interests Whigs grew concerned that an incoming Tory government might support agitation for further factory reform. This might affect a much greater proportion of manufacturers than the existing act. Those supporting reform of working conditions had realised that there were many industries other than textiles and that children and young people in these industries had no protection from bad working practices.

On 4 August 1840, Ashley moved an address to the Crown for an inquiry into the various branches of trade and manufacture in which numbers of children work together that were not covered by existing legislation. In his speech he outlined horrifying abuses that he had discovered across a range of industries. Many who did not support Ashley's calls for reform saw his request for an inquiry as an opportunity to distract him from campaigning. This included members of the government. On its behalf, an under-secretary at the Home Office cordially extended the government's aid to collecting the information that Ashley was requesting.

After a short discussion, and shocked by the speech they had just heard, members of the House of Commons supported Ashley's call to petition the queen to set up a Royal Commission, without a formal vote needing to be taken. Included in the list of industries to be investigated was mining.

CHAPTER 3

Knights in Shining Armour
The work of the Children's Employment Commission

We work from six in the morning till seven or eight at night. The
time is long and the work very hard indeed, the sad, tiring sort and
I feel very glad when over.

Ann David, 13, haulier of skips

Queen Victoria established the Royal Commission in October 1840. Lord
Ashley was made its president, supported by four Commissioners with a
variety of skills and considerable experience who were recommended for
appointment by the then Home Secretary, the Marquis of Normanby. The
Commission was tasked to inquire into the employment of the children of
the poorer classes in mines and collieries and the various branches of trade
and manufacturing in which numbers of children worked together which
were not included in the laws regulating the employment of children and
young persons in mills and factories. It became known as the Children's
Employment Commission.

The definition of a child restricted the inquiry to those under thirteen.
In February 1841, following a request by the House of Commons, the
scope was extended to cover young people meaning that the age limit
became eighteen.

Ashley had no influence over the selection of the Commissioners. His
years of calls for factory reform had not endeared him to the many Whigs
whose fortune had been made from manufacturing. They regarded the
spotlight that factory reformers wanted to shine on conditions in industry
as unwarranted interference that would replicate Sadler's approach and
deliberately seek out extreme examples to present as a norm.

To guard against an unbalanced or emotive investigation being carried
out the four Commissioners selected were capable of weighing evidence,
balancing conflicting points of view, making valid comparison across
industries and understanding the business perspective of employers.

Thomas Tooke was an influential economist who had given evidence
to several official committees. Doctor Thomas Southwood Smith was a
prominent public health campaigner who had trained at Edinburgh and

practised in the East End of London. He could pronounce definitively whether conditions experienced by children in mines and other industries were harmful to their health. Both men had substantial experience of royal Commissions as they had been Commissioners for the 1833 factory inquiry and actively involved in producing a balanced report to counter the bad impression created by some of Sadler's emotive evidence.

They were joined by Leonard Horner and Robert Saunders, two of the factory inspectors appointed as a consequence of the 1833 Factory Act. Horner, who had gathered evidence for the factory inquiry, covered northern England and Lancashire. Saunders was responsible for Yorkshire and the east of England. Their inclusion enabled the Commission to evaluate working practices and conditions against those found in the textile factories. It may also have been an attempt to distract them from their inspection role. Horner was considered by some factory owners to be more thorough and persistent in his inspections and enforcement than they thought he should be.

The Letters Patent setting up the Royal Commission outlined the work required. It was to collect information about the time allowed each day for meals, the actual state, condition and treatment of the children and the effects of employment on their morals and their bodily health. Evidence was to be obtained not only from within the industry but also from a range of external observers such as magistrates, ministers and local officials. The Commission was not given any remit to identify problems or propose solutions. Its role was confined to gathering facts, not forming any judgement on industrial practices.

The Commissioners were tasked to report back with as little delay as was consistent with a due discharge of their duties. This had the potential to take several years. The scope of the inquiry was wide, encompassing mines, collieries and all manufacturing not covered by existing factory legislation. When the House of Commons supported Ashley's petition the motivation of some MPs was to keep him occupied by a large and apparently important investigation on a topic that greatly interested him. Those opposed to the reform of workers' conditions would have hoped that Ashley would fall into the trap of spending so long investigating that he had no time to agitate for change.

The four Commissioners were supported by sub-Commissioners who were appointed by the Home Secretary to carry out the inquiry in the field. The first six, James Mitchell, John Kennedy, Samuel Scriven, Leonard Stewart, Jelinger Symons and Richard Grainger, were appointed in November 1840 and allocated to districts thought most likely to benefit from their experience.

In January 1841, Thomas Tancred, Robert Franks, Frederick Roper, William Wood, John Leifchild and Anthony Austin were appointed. By this time it was apparent that the volume of work was much greater than had been envisaged and by March 1841 a further eight were in post: Thomas Martin, Elijah Waring, Major Burns, Richard Horne, John Fellows, Charles Barham, Hugh Jones and Rhys Jones. The latter two were recruited for their ability to speak Welsh as it was felt important for the inquiry to be able to hear directly the evidence of those giving it.

The letter appointing Truro doctor Charles Barham, who investigated the tin mines in Cornwall, survived amongst his personal papers and reveals that the sub-Commissioners received a fee of £100 (worth about £4,500 today) for their task. It was more than two years disposable income for a coal miner.

Most of the sub-Commissioners have receded into history and it is difficult to identify information about them. They appear to represent a cross section of prosperous society and had a range of professional expertise. Some were known to the establishment because of their participation in earlier Commissions and investigations. The group included at least four doctors, two barristers, three businessmen, a clergyman and two writers. Many were relatively young men. Some were under forty and several were around thirty. This suggests that some would have seen the appointment as an opportunity to develop their reputation and career. Taken as a group, the sub-Commissioners had a broad spectrum of expertise but with a number of them being businessmen or from prosperous industrial families there may have been some bias in the selection towards men who might be presumed to be receptive to an employer's point of view.

The locality reports demonstrate that sub-Commissioners approached their task with varying degrees of commitment and diligence and some investigated in greater depth than others, taking pains to familiarise themselves with the lives of the mining communities. Some focussed their inquiries firmly in the sphere of their professional interest and may not have considered the breadth of the situation as fully as they might. The sub-Commissioners who discovered women toiling underground spontaneously extended their investigation to cover this work though they could have ignored it because females over eighteen did not fall within the scope of the Royal Commission.

✳   ✳   ✳

Cambridge-educated Jelinger Cookson Symons was born into a clerical family in Berkshire. In 1837 he was appointed an Assistant Commissioner for the inquiry into the condition of hand-loom weavers and manufacturers. When appointed to the inquiry into mines he was training to become a barrister. It is likely that this training accounts for the amount of detail he was able to draw out of those he interviewed. The long statements he obtained from workers and children suggest that he had a personality that readily put people at ease.

Religion, morality, education and safety feature strongly in his report though he did not stint on investigating the subjects in which he had lesser interest. His report for Yorkshire was one of the most detailed, combining 300 witness statements with the measurements of more than 200 children and personal observation of mines and of workers' living conditions. He recorded the evidence of fifty-six females.

Samuel Swain Scriven was a doctor and future Fellow of the Royal College of Surgeons. He avoided any temptation to concentrate on medical issues and said surprisingly little on this topic. He adopted a proactive method of obtaining evidence, dressing in collier clothes and going down several pits to interview children in their work environment. He believed that this approach had enabled him to write more accurately about what he found and to defend his statements if called on to do so. He was initially sent to North Staffordshire and took over some districts in Yorkshire when sub-Commissioner Wood became too ill to continue.

Robert Hugh Franks was a businessman. He had kept two hat shops in London, one in Regent Street and one in the City. The businesses failed. He had spent time in prison for a libel on the clerk of the Fishmongers' Company. Whether this was known to those who appointed him is unclear. The Marquis of Londonderry, who seems to have regarded the hard-hitting published report as a personal affront, subsequently publicised these salacious facts to try to undermine the credibility and integrity of all the sub-Commissioners and the evidence they produced.

Franks was extremely thorough in his investigations. In Scotland he interviewed 431 witnesses including 123 females. He commissioned reports from doctors and made detailed studies of education, crime and drinking. He then moved to South Wales to assist Rhys Jones who was making slow progress. There he interviewed 454 witnesses, many of whom worked in the iron industry rather than in the mines. On occasions he tried to ascertain whether there were similar practices in Wales to ones he had seen in Scotland. This provided valuable comparative information but meant that he did not always ascertain the most relevant information about Welsh mining.

Franks reported a substantial lack of co-operation with his investigation from owners in Scotland and drew attention to his inability to take evidence on oath as he thought this would have improved its reliability.

William Rayner Wood was from a Manchester industrial family. He was at the beginning of an illustrious career in which he became a director of a

Manchester Savings Bank, an administrator at Manchester College, a training establishment for Unitarian ministers, a Justice of the Peace and the Deputy Lieutenant of Lancashire. He was a member of the influential Manchester Statistical Society.

His investigation was in the Bradford and Leeds areas where female workers underground were not common and he only interviewed two. After meeting nine-year-old Mary Ann Lund, who pointed out that her family also contained two great lads who worked, he immediately considered the economic necessity for taking young children underground, and re-interviewed the pit steward about Mary Ann and her six-year-old brother. He formed intelligent conclusions about education and identified the ignorance of the prosperous about the reality of miners' lives. He reported that the condition of mining families would be far worse if women were not at home to look after their families. This view had been formed through discussions with middle-class witnesses.

Lancashire was investigated by barrister John Lawson Kennedy. He was the son of a respected Manchester engineer whose family wealth had been built by supplying machinery to the local mills. He decided that the best way to establish a correct impression of conditions was to speak to practical men, and those engaged in mining. He recorded the evidence of 116 witnesses, went down some pits and visited miners' houses. He does not appear to have been at ease when interviewing children and gleaned little information from them, though he was comfortable about raising questions of propriety with married women. Discussions with owners and managers form a large part of his evidence.

For an area with as many mines as Lancashire, Kennedy's enquiries were light in comparison with the painstaking approach of Franks and Symons but he came to similar conclusions. His report was characterised by hostility towards miners as a group and he portrayed them in a very negative way.

It is possible that Kennedy lost or discarded some evidence. His report quoted people whose statements were not included with the published witness statements. He stated that he had suppressed part of the evidence of one owner as unfit for publication, indicating that he was not averse to censorship.

The Commissioners were keen to ensure that comparable information was obtained for all areas and provided detailed instructions for the sub-Commissioners, requesting them to focus their work under key headings. The intention was that this would optimise their use of their time. The Commission wanted to know the age and numbers of children employed, their hours of work and arrangements for meals, how the children were hired and their working conditions including accidents, details of holidays and wages, how the children were treated, the effect of work on their physical and moral condition and the comparative condition with children in other occupations.

Sub-Commissioners were tasked to verify the information that they gathered and to avoid citing isolated examples of problems or using extreme examples to create a bad impression. As very little was known about the mining industry they were empowered to use their own discretion to follow through any other aspects of the industry that they identified as necessary, to enable them to present a rounded report.

The Commissioners wrote to all mine owners explaining the purpose of the inquiry and asking them to complete and return a schedule about the number and gender of those employed in their pits. They hoped that being open about the purpose of the inquiry would gain the co-operation of owners in identifying practices within the industry. The schedule they sent separated out males and females. It was the only aspect of the planning of the investigation that made any reference to adult women.

Despite all the effort that went into planning, adjustments had to be made as work progressed. William Wood caught a severe chill and his outstanding work was split between Symons, who was covering the coal and steel industries in the southern part of Yorkshire, and Scriven who had completed his work in North Staffordshire. The investigations of Rhys Jones in South Wales were slow to progress and his effort was supplemented by Franks who had a much more robust approach. When the individual reports were being collated in October 1841 Joseph Fletcher, the secretary to the Commission, spent a week reinspecting mines to the east of Manchester when it became apparent that Kennedy's inquiries in the area had been cursory. This district lies between west Lancashire and west Yorkshire where women worked underground and the commissioners probably suspected that women worked here also. Fletcher's visit confirmed that they did not.

From January through to summer 1841, the sub-Commissioners travelled through their areas interviewing witnesses. This was the early stage of developing railway mania. George Bradshaw had already published an early edition of his railway guide and it is likely that some sub-Commissioners travelled by rail for at least part of their journeys. The other methods of transport at their disposal were stagecoaches, hackney cabs or horses if they were proficient riders.

Accompanying the sub-Commissioners were clerks who were able to take down witness testimonies using shorthand, a method of recording speech by capturing letters or sounds on paper as strokes or symbols. When its notation has been memorised words can be recorded accurately at a normal talking speed. Shorthand was taught to students as part of a university education and would have been known by those who worked in government service. Isaac Pitman had introduced a new system of shorthand in 1837. To a competent user, Pitman's system gave a further speed advantage by making vowels optional if a word could be represented accurately by consonants only. It is possible that some of the clerks had learned to use this notation.

* * *

During the inquiry sub-Commissioners collectively interviewed several thousand witnesses. They achieved this by visiting mines where they were able to speak to numbers of people on the same day, and in some cases they spoke to groups together. They gave more attention to the small collieries where the coal seams were thin, quickly realising that practices in these were very different to those that prevailed where the seams were thick.

Their approach meant that a wide range of views was obtained from those within the industry and from interested observers. Sometimes sub-Commissioners invited local professionals, usually doctors, to accompany them on their visits and to comment on the health of the children.

There were difficulties in gathering accurate evidence. The four Commissioners had been given the power to interview witnesses under oath but this did not extend to the sub-Commissioners who were, on occasions, sceptical about what they were told but unable to probe its accuracy. Some pit owners refused to co-operate with the inquiry and would not make themselves available for interview or complete the forms sent out by the Commissioners.

The arrival of investigators does not seem to have attracted universal coverage in local newspapers but its potential implications were known to workers by word of mouth and it was anticipated that children would be stopped from working, raising fears about loss of wages. Margaret Drysdale told Franks that the lassies would tell him they all liked the work fine as they thought he was going to take them out of the pits. Some workers may have been threatened with this outcome by colliery officials to discourage them from reporting bad conditions. Legislation had followed the factory inquiry and it was not unreasonable to suppose that Parliament might intervene again if bad practices were discovered.

The coal industry, like others, was in a period of depression in 1841. Workers reliant on their employer for income would be unwilling to jeopardise it, even if this meant lying or avoiding the opportunity to tell their story. They may have been intimidated to see a clerk recording everything they said and concerned about whether this would be reported back to their employer. Women may have been instructed by their husband and children ordered by both parents not to speak to the inspector when he came, or, if they had to, to tell him how much they enjoyed pit work.

Large owners and companies tended to be outwardly helpful. Employers who were part of the establishment would find it difficult to ignore an inquiry commissioned by the queen. Many large enterprises were well organised and able to respond to questions without difficulty. Several had set up schools for the children of mining families and provided medical care for sick miners. They also had fewer concerns about the investigation because they mined thick seams, where the employment of young children was rare or was being actively phased out.

The majority of mines were supervised by a manager or steward and owners had varying degrees of interest in anything beyond the money the coal made for them. As witnesses, many of the colliery officials appear unduly positive about conditions in their own pit which is unsurprising as owners would not want to discover that they had reported bad practices. Some stressed that problems observed at other pits did not happen in theirs, implying that unlike other collieries they operated high standards. They were often critical of conditions in other industries, stating that they would be unwilling for their daughters to work in those. A few had daughters working at the pit, though sometimes above ground.

Some pit managers were prepared to try and hoodwink the inspectors. Symons maintained the anonymity of a miner from a wet pit at Mirfield who reported being ordered by the banksman to pump out the water before Symons arrived and to work in a dry spot whilst he inspected. Others lied. Symons highlighted the evidence of Harriet Morton about the number and ages of girls working at Webster and Peace's pit, which distinctly contradicted the more favourable picture painted by its owner, Thomas Peace. Harriet named and gave the ages of seven girls working at the pit, the eldest being almost fifteen. Peace said that there were three girls employed and girls were always dismissed at thirteen.

Disorganisation, poor records and low levels of literacy could account for the non-completion of returns by some pits but some provided misleading data. Franks reported adjusting a number of returns from the pits he visited to a more accurate figure.

The sub-Commissioners were not easily fooled by owners and managers who were recognised as having a vested interest in the inquiry. They were more susceptible to the views that they obtained from middle-class observers especially as these tended to corroborate each other. The general conclusions that they drew about female miners as coarse, and lacking in womanly feelings or domestic skills stemmed from evidence provided by middle-class witnesses.

Within the industry and external to it, some middle-class witnesses had motivations that led them to give evidence that was less accurate than it might have been. Several appear to have deliberately painted a very dismal picture of females working in mines because they wanted to see the practice end. This demonstrates that not all businessmen were opposed to external interference in how a business was run. Small enterprises found that local market mechanisms could perpetuate practices that they found repugnant. If one pit tried to stop a worker taking his daughter underground the outcome could be that the worker moved to a pit where the manager had fewer scruples.

One of the most notable examples of the provision of misleading evidence for altruistic reasons was John Thorneley, a Justice of the Peace and a mine manager for forty years. Symons met him the same day that he discovered four girls working without tops. His opening question was about how women dressed underground. Thorneley may have picked up a cue about what the shocked investigator was prepared to believe and confirmed that young women frequently worked half-dressed, that modesty was something they knew in name only and that bastardy was frequent. He was also very disparaging about the ability of mining women to look after a family. The rest of his evidence reveals a man who was caring and knowledgeable about the mining industry and supportive of high standards. He concluded with the hope that before he died he would have the satisfaction of seeing the employment of females in coal pits prevented and entirely done away with.

Some clergy, teachers and relieving officers may have given evidence that was tinted with envy. A mining family with several members working could earn up to £3 a week, which was more than the stipends of some curates or the salaries of some officials. The lifestyles of mining families were seen to include copious drinking, raucous behaviour and non-attendance at church. It would not be surprising if people who saw themselves as leading good moral lives on less income were unduly harsh about mining families and the abilities of the women in these households.

The evidence of a few witnesses is so clearly supposition or uncorroborated opinion that it provides only an uncomfortable insight into the preoccupations and fantasies of people who would have considered themselves scions of respectability.

Where it was based on knowledge, some middle-class witnesses provided valuable insights. Michael Sadler, a Barnsley doctor, accurately analysed that it was the exhausting nature of the work that made it difficult for mining women to excel at domestic duties and criticised the practice rather than the women. Others placed what were considered undesirable characteristics in context and acknowledged that the values of mining women were no different to those who worked in other occupations.

Sub-Commissioners obtained evidence from miners of both sexes. Men held a variety of views about women working underground. Some claimed it would be impossible for the family to manage without the female's work. Other men, often the ones who were not maintaining a large family or who had several sons, were adamant that mining was no work for a lassie and that women should not be allowed underground. It may not have been altruism that guided their view. Ending female work underground could be financially advantageous for those with sons available to fill the resulting vacancies.

Particularly interesting was the evidence of a small number of miners such as Samuel Well, David Swallow and John Oldham whose under-standing of the industry they worked in was far in advance of that of many pit owners and managers. In 1842, David Swallow began a long and respected career as a leader of mining trades unions.

The most important testimony about the lives of female miners was provided by the women and girls who worked underground. Around 500 females feature in the Commission evidence. Most worked under-ground, some were in surface jobs and others no longer mined. Some gave detailed statements, others left only the silent testimony of measurements on a chart.

The women and girls who spoke to the sub-Commissioners tended to be self-selected, as most only interviewed those who approached them. Some may have been put forward by pit officials as the least likely to make indiscreet comments. Some may have told the sub-Commissioner what they thought he wanted to hear. Any girl interviewed in earshot of a colliery official would have been very circumspect in her reply.

Some young witnesses had been coached. At the Meal Hill pit in Hepworth it was obvious that Mary Holmes had been crammed with her evidence when she confirmed that she would rather be in the pit where she was thrashed sometimes and worked in the wet than do anything else. Mary's evidence contradicted not only what Symons had observed but also what other children told him about conditions in that pit.

Amongst the female witnesses the sub-Commissioners met some very well-presented, intelligent, articulate women and girls who conducted themselves with dignity and propriety. This was at variance with what many witnesses told them about mining women, their attitudes and their capabilities. The sub-Commissioners made no attempt to ascertain why the views of many witnesses were so different from what they were seeing and hearing from the females they spoke to. Those who spotted the contra-diction dealt with it by concluding that some of the women were exceptional. Symons drew attention to four. Kennedy considered the evidence of a dozen females to be reliable.

Some of the conclusions presented by the sub-Commissioners about female miners were the reason why this group of women were widely portrayed in newspaper coverage and parliamentary debate as brutish, degenerate creatures whose innocence became corrupted by their surroundings.

Witness statements that formed the basis of the sub-Commissioners' views were published verbatim along with the official report from the Royal Commission. Analysing these statements, whilst being conscious of the biases that may have affected them, indicates that the lives and capabilities of female miners in the mid-nineteenth century were very different to the way they were generally portrayed in 1842 and how they have tended to be regarded ever since.

CHAPTER 4

The Un-Magical Mystery Tour
The places where women worked underground

On short shifts I work from eight in the morning till six at night; on long ones until ten at night; occasionally we work all night. When at night-work, from six at night till eight and ten in the morning.

Margaret Hipps, 17, putter

The sub-Commissioners discovered four areas where women and girls worked underground, a few areas where the practise had almost died out, some places where they worked at the pit head but not underground and regions where they had not been involved with mining for some years. In the vast, thick-seamed coalfields of Durham and Tyneside underground work by females barely fell within living memory.

Women were an integral part of underground work in east Scotland, west Lancashire, west Yorkshire and south Wales. Many of the pits where they worked shared characteristics of thin seams and lack of investment in underground infrastructure. By 1841, women working underground and bad conditions were found together.

All four regions had an individual profile of female employment. Within the regions were small localities where the pattern of work was more similar to practises in a different region rather than to ones that prevailed a few miles away. Flockton near Huddersfield appeared in some respects more like Lancashire than the rest of Yorkshire. A few mining families in Scotland seemed more akin to families in the mill towns of Yorkshire than to their neighbours. There were some similarities between Scotland and Wales in the employment of very young girls and older women.

A few weeks after the sub-Commissioners interviewed most of their witnesses, census enumerators blanketed the country. The census that was taken on 6 June 1841 aimed to produce a very detailed picture of the population. Unlike the four previous censuses, which counted numbers of households and the number of people living within them, the intention in 1841 was to record the names of individuals and basic information about them such as their occupation.

Some of the witnesses to the Commission can be traced to the census, which reveals their personal situation within their household. Using the census and the Commission evidence together produces a more comprehensive picture of the women's role in coal mining than is apparent when the documents are considered separately.

1. Scotland

In Scotland the pits where women worked underground were located along both shores of the Firth of Forth. The coal belt began to the east of Edinburgh, and covered Tranent, Dalkeith, Edinburgh, Bathgate, Falkirk, Linlithgow, Kilsyth, Stirling, Alloa, Dunfermline, Kircaldy and Weymss. There was also a small amount of female work in Peebleshire.

The Duke of Hamilton, the Marquis of Lothian and the Earl of Elgin employed large numbers of women in their mines as did some coal companies. A Scottish MP, Captain Weymss, employed twenty-five women and girls at his large colliery in Fife. Reverend Beresford reported thirty-one women and girls in his pits in West Linton. Twelve of them were under thirteen. In these pits there were almost twice as many females as males. When there was no mechanised lifting gear two people were required to carry to the surface the coal a hewer could cut in a shift.

Reverend Berrisford appears to have been an absentee leaseholder so it is not clear whether he knew that his mines were employing the youngest female miners in Scotland. Franks spoke to bearer Margaret Leveston, recording her age as six. Jesse Coutte, Mary Neilson and Margaret Watson confirmed that starting work at six or seven was normal. Jane Peacock Watson, an adult bearer, said that even six-year-olds did much to relieve the burthen.

There were almost 120 pits around the Forth and the employment returns provided to Franks showed that females worked at the majority of them. Approximately one-tenth did not employ females and a few others reported that they were trying to eradicate female labour or restrict it to work above ground. These all tended to be small or medium-sized. The Duke of Buccleugh employed less than a hundred men and Mr Ramsey recorded just over a hundred so the impact of removing women from these pits would not have had wide ramifications.

When the exclusions took place some miners moved to pits where their women were still welcomed. Many returned within a few years, when they discovered that they could earn as much money without the women in the modernised pits. Turnover of workers declined and as there were not many women seeking work at any one time those who wanted a job were usually able to find a post in service.

In other pits females formed between a third and a half of the workforce. The higher the proportion of women the more likely it was that they were carrying coal on their backs. Females comprised around thirty percent of workers in some of the pits in Alloa, an area where they stopped working when they married. This created vacancies that unmarried girls filled as the biggest difference between Alloa and other areas is that more girls under eighteen were employed than adult females. In most pits the number of adult women exceeded the number of under eighteens. Men electing to keep married women out of the mines increased the turnover of female workers rather than reducing the number who were employed.

Females comprised approximately a quarter of the workforce in the pits around Dunfermline though one reported forty-two percent. It is unclear whether this is a genuine reflection of the position or whether these were figures which Franks suspected of being inaccurate. The proportion of females in the area seems low when compared to the situation elsewhere.

Contradicting the evidence given by some older witnesses the census suggests that the practice of men marrying at a very young age to obtain a bearer was rare. Most young married miners, male and female, were in their twenties rather than their teens. Substantial numbers of unmarried boys in their late teens and early twenties lived and worked with their parents. They were matched by a number of unmarried women of similar age also working with a family member.

Throughout the region a number of females were recorded as drawers or putters, confirming the assertions of some owners and managers that the labour-intensive practise of carrying coals on the back was being eliminated, roads constructed and carts introduced.

Using the census to draw conclusions about the condition of Scottish mining families is problematic because it gives no indication of the health status of those enumerated and in some districts only the head of the household had an occupation recorded. In the Edinburgh districts of Millerhall and New Craighall the enumerator was assiduous in listing the roles of everyone in the household. A few Commission witnesses lived in these two these districts and Franks interviewed the manager of New Craighall colliery where some of them worked. Their evidence provides a small amount of supplementary information to suggest context to the census records.

Fifty-two females from Millerhall were miners and came from forty-seven families. Their ages ranged from sixty-five to ten. Eighteen came from just five families. In New Craighall twenty-five female miners came from fourteen households with ages ranging from twelve to fifty.

Over a third of these families included a married woman who appears to have been looking after the home, including families with no-one else in the household to help the head at the pit. The mines where some of these families worked had ended coal bearing a few years earlier and brought in carts and horses. This meant that men needed one or two assistants rather than the entire family.

Improved haulage underground led to increased output, which translated into more pay for the miners. Some could afford to pay for others to help them and allow their wives to remain at home. Agnes and Margaret Phinn, who worked to support their widowed mother, were hired by James Ross, a twenty-nine-year-old miner with a wife and young child.

In both districts the majority of female miners were young adults; unmarried daughters of the miners they worked for, or working on their own account to support widowed or infirm parents. It is likely that the tendency for adult female miners to be unmarried rather than married was a recent development. It would have been more predominant in mines where coal was moved in trucks.

In families where the head remained in good health there are hints that a few mining families enjoyed a reasonable standard of living because all able-bodied members continued to work rather than some of the women remaining at home. In New Craighall seven members of the Gray family mined. Seven of nine members of the Brown family were miners and a family servant looked after two young children. Both families included three female miners.

In Millerhall, seventeen-year-old Agnes Moffatt came from a family of six in which all worked as miners. Her evidence suggests that her father was working and hints that she and her two sisters were afforded no say in how they earned their living. All five members of the Jack family, including two women, were miners. Seventeen-year-old Margaret said that the work was not her choice but her parents' will. A female servant lived with the family. Neither Agnes, Margaret nor her brother James indicated that their families depended on their wages.

Some of these trends were replicated elsewhere. The census shows that Margaret Watson of Bothwell, the only female in a family of twelve, came from a household in which everyone was listed as a miner, including two five-year-old boys. It is difficult to believe that this family needed a wage from everyone.

James Archibald who worked with his father, brother and sister said that mother now stayed at home as they had no need for her labour. Jane Wood, a coal bearer for thirty years, no longer worked because her family had no need for her to assist them.

If a reasonable lifestyle could be obtained by families who enjoyed good health and worked in pits that used trucks, the converse applied when the head of the family was not well enough to bring in an income. Many female miners were in this category. Margaret Harper, Nancy Morrison and Elizabeth Selkirk were amongst a procession of girls who reported fathers unable to work because of 'bad breath'. Jane Brown, Margaret Crookston and Isabella Read had already lost their fathers. Watching helplessly as a husband or father gasped for breath or coughed and spit mucus as black as ink from his lungs was common among mining families.

Bad breath was a serious but undefined respiratory condition whose cause has now been identified as silica dust. Silica is a component of hard rocks such as granite, which are found around the River Forth. As hewers inhaled dust from the rocks they hacked, their lung tissue was pierced by sharp shards of silica. Although the lungs healed, scar tissue would eventually form leaving them less flexible and efficient than they should be. Asthmatic attacks and bronchitis were early signs of lung damage. In time more serious complaints such as silicosis could develop, gradually reducing the functioning of the lungs and making breathing difficult. The outcome could be lung or heart failure. A miner with lung disease would also be susceptible to other infections.

If the family was lucky a man would manage to work until there was a son able to get coals. Mary MacQueen's fourteen-year-old brother could cut coal by the time their father's health deteriorated past the point of being able to work. A young teenager was unlikely to cut as much coal as an adult man, which would reduce family income and intensify any poverty the family was already experiencing.

As fathers became too ill to work children were contracted to work for the mine owner, often on the mother's account, either alone or in small family groups to earn whatever they could. Some mothers worked alongside the children. Many were unable to assist as their own health had been compromised by years of work underground. Others had to stay at home to nurse their ailing husbands and look after younger children.

Twelve-year-old Janet Moffatt from New Craighall and two sisters worked as miners to help their widowed mother and young brother. In Dunfermline, sixteen-year-old Helen Spowort helped to maintain her widowed stepmother who was too ill to work. Without Helen's work the family would have been put out of their home, which appears to have been a tied house provided by the colliery.

Working to support elderly or ailing parents fell disproportionately to younger children in families as older ones had moved on and had families of their own. Jane Snaddon was the last child out of twelve at home and the parish had refused her aged parents any assistance.

When parents died young the disadvantage lay with older girls who had to work to maintain younger children. It was not uncommon for female miners to live in households with their siblings when both parents were dead. Seventeen-year-old Janet Borrowman, her two elder brothers and two sisters lived together in one room at Grange Pans. This may have affected the marriage prospects of some girls through refusal to abandon a parent or reluctance on the part of a suitor to assume responsibility for a girl's dependants.

The census shows that Scotland had some of the oldest female miners in the country. Sixty-five-year-old Margaret Banks worked in Sir John Hope's collieries at Millerhall. In Dunfermline Sarah Burt, also sixty-five, was a coal bearer for Alexander Penman whilst his wife remained at home with their young children. Sarah lived in the same household as this family but it is not clear whether they were related. Another sixty-five-year-old was Violet Ross who acted as bearer for her husband at Dalkeith. Jannet Harguson, aged seventy-four, lived alone and was working as a miner in Tranent.

Age did not feature in Franks' report. One former bearer was reported as working until she was sixty-six, but this appeared exceptional. The picture that emerged of mining in the east of Scotland was of an unhealthy industry sustained by juvenile workers of both sexes who married young, had large families and replicated the cycle of ill health and deprivation generation by generation.

The reality was more complicated and varied between districts. The mining industry was modernising its methods and replacing the labour-intensive activity of coal bearing with trucks and mechanisation in pits where this was practical. This afforded some married women the opportunity to remain at home. Neither Franks nor anyone else identified that a large proportion of female labour below ground was provided by un-married adults. The belief that the females who worked in mines were married women and young girls was the view that prevailed in 1841.

2. Lancashire

Moving south to Lancashire female employment underground had very different characteristics. The practise was confined to the north and west of Manchester in an area that included Worsley, Bolton, Wigan and St Helens. Unfortunately, Kennedy made a cursory investigation in the area and did not interview many witnesses. This makes it more difficult to identify and understand any local variation.

What he did do was tabulate all the collieries that provided no figures so it is possible to ascertain that there were almost 200 pits in the area. Less than a third of them sent in any returns. The non-compliance was not confined to the areas where women were employed. There is no reason to consider that the returns received do not provide a representative picture of mining in the area.

More than a quarter of west Lancashire's pits were located around Wigan and were medium or small. St Helens had twenty and Bolton fifteen. The biggest single employer of miners was the Bridgewater Estate which employed over 1,000 workers at Worsley near Manchester.

The estate had recently instituted a programme of modernisation and banned the employment of married women and girls under twelve. This was reflected in its returns, which showed that females formed nine per cent of the workforce. Across the larger employers females comprised between ten and thirty per cent of workers. Often there were more adult women than girls under eighteen and in a number of pits there were relatively few girls under thirteen.

Benjamin Berry referred to a pit that employed more females than males. This is not borne out by any returns and was unlikely to be the situation in anything but the smallest pit where a man working in a family unit could be assisted by a wife and daughters.

Several witnesses believed the number of females working underground was high because miners preferred to have women and girls drawing their coal. Females had no ambitions to hew coal whereas an adolescent boy was always keen to try. In Spring 1841, mining was in a depression and strikes were taking place in some pits. Miners who were afraid of competition from adolescent males must have been concerned about their own prospects of continued employment. If women were being taken underground in preference to boys, the motivation may have been to restrict the supply of skilled workers, as this would help to maintain wage levels.

Some women were late recruits to the industry having worked in cotton mills. This explains why there were was a preponderance of adult women in the mines of Lancashire. Miners were reputed to seek out factory girls for wives because of their superior homemaking talents. As miners commanded higher wages than other types of workers, mill girls would be pleased to have a miner as their suitor. It could mean a more secure future, especially when the cotton trade was slack and wages fell. Betty Harris and Jane Sym were factory girls who moved into mining and drew coal for their men. The reality of working underground became apparent later. Jane's husband drank her wages. Betty was beaten many a time by her 'fella' for not being able to work fast enough.

When an adult woman worked with her husband their daughters often worked in textiles, although sons were taken to the pit. Drawer Mary Glover thought mining was too hard for girls and her daughter Margaret worked as a cloth piecer. Miner John Oldham was determined that his daughters would not work in mining in his lifetime.

When a miner found a girl to draw for him they were reputed to live together until they became parents. It was known as 'living tally'. The census includes a few young and childless mining couples, but they have the same surname and appear to be married. It is possible that an unmarried couple would have chosen to disguise their status for the enumerator.

Some females worked for a family member and others were employed by the pit. The latter were from mining families and introduced by their fathers. Alice Hatherton and her sisters, Betty Houghton, and Eliza and Mary Ann Hunt were daughters of colliery officials and worked underground. Alice Singleton and Ellen Yates worked for their parents. Alice appears to have been working as part of a family group.

Extremes of age amongst female miners were rare. The youngest girl interviewed by Kennedy was nine and he spoke with no woman over forty. The census shows that mining families usually had one adult woman at home keeping house. It is likely that by the time a pit woman was forty she had taken over the domestic responsibilities from an aged mother.

3. Yorkshire

Female involvement in mining in west Yorkshire was a complex situation with striking differences between areas only a few miles apart. Working underground had become mainly confined to an area that hugged the Pennines where the coal seams were thin. It began at Halifax and snaked round to cover Brighouse, Huddersfield, Holmfirth, Barnsley and Stocksbridge to the north of Sheffield.

The returns provided to Wood have disappeared. Symons collated the returns for eighty pits but did not name them or identify what was missing, so it is not possible to explore what was happening in localities.

According to the returns less than 400 females worked and there were no extremes of age. There were thirty-five girls under ten and eighty-six women over eighteen. Only thirty-three pits employed females and of these only four employed more than ten adult women. Only in one of these did they make up more than ten percent of the total workforce. No pit had more than twenty adult women.

Female mining in parts of west Yorkshire displayed similarity to Lancashire a few decades earlier. In Bradford, Halifax and Huddersfield, where a mechanised woollen industry had become established, women went to work in the mills when they became old enough to work twelve-hour shifts. Those from large families were replaced underground by a younger sibling. At Hepworth, fourteen-year-old Mary Holmes was a middle child in a family of fourteen. Her older sisters had moved from mining to marriage, service or the mills. It is likely that Mary was waiting for a place in a factory as the family had younger children who could take her place.

Even in districts without much alternative employment for women it was becoming the norm for a girl to stop working underground when she was fourteen. If families did not find other jobs for their daughters some owners took the initiative and dismissed them or only allowed them to remain as a favour to needy families.

A few pits had only one female working. The most interesting was seventeen-year-old Patience Kershaw at Booth Town Pit in Halifax where she worked alongside twenty boys moving coal and fifteen naked miners. Patience was one of nine children supporting a widowed mother and a sick sister. Younger sisters had left for jobs in a mill, which makes it curious that she continued to move coals.

The treatment meted out by some of the men and boys she worked with would today be regarded as workplace harassment. She was sometimes struck on her back if she was not not quick enough and the boys pulled her about and took liberties with her though she did not specify what these were.

Scriven described Patience as a deplorable object, barely removed from idiocy and also as an ignorant, filthy, ragged and deplorable looking object and such a one as the uncivilised natives of the prairies would be shocked to look upon. Usually he was caring and compassionate towards females and notes he made about individual women were factual rather than emotive. This suggests that Scriven, a doctor, may have used the word idiocy in its medical sense. At the time, those with mental problems were graded by terms such as moron, imbecile and idiot, depending on the nature and severity of their condition.

Scriven may have diagnosed that Patience had very mild learning disabilities. Such a condition would have made it more difficult for her to find employment in a mill because of prejudice and a possible need for supervision. Moving coal carts demanded only strength. Operating machinery in a mill needed judgement also. It would also explain the horseplay to which Patience was subjected to by the boys in the mine. Those with disabilities were regarded as legitimate sources of entertainment by many of the able-bodied.

If Patience did have a mild learning disability it raises questions about family attitudes towards a child or sibling with mental disability. Her siblings were prepared for a sister whose legs were prone to swelling to remain at home, but expected Patience to work in a hostile environment where she was the only female.

At Flockton near Huddersfield and Silkstone near Barnsley the Lancashire practise of a woman acting as a hurrier for her husband was mentioned several times. The returns suggest that the practise was very limited by 1841. None of the women involved were interviewed and some witnesses gave examples that were not contemporary. The change appears to be very recent and collective thinking amongst mining communities that females should not work underground unless the family could not mange without their work may have been the cause of the decline.

When girls over fourteen remained underground particular reasons were cited for this. At the Gawber Pit in Barnsley the Eggley sisters, and the Gooder sisters came from families who had no sons old enough to work. When two helpers were needed to move coal, an older girl might have to remain in the mine to work alongside a younger child. This appears to have been the situation with seventeen-year-old Ann Gooder who was hired out with her twelve-year-old sister, Maria.

It is noticeable from the census that the families who adhered to the tradition of all able-bodied members working underground were usually living in mixed communities amongst factory workers and tradesmen and working in smaller pits. In such surroundings the collective opinion of neighbours and colleagues would not be strong enough to influence their behaviour.

Ann Ambler, Mary Ann Lund, Mary and Ruth Barrett and Sarah Jowett all came from families where most of the family worked, including families where six- and eight-year-old boys were working. Wood analysed the Lund family's income and concluded that they ought to have been able to manage without the earnings of Mary Ann and her young brother.

When most members worked, mining families could enjoy a good standard of living which was reflected in their food, drink and clothes. Others made the choice to keep females out of mining and may have lived more frugally in order to achieve this.

The judgement of all three sub-Commissioners who covered Yorkshire was that the reason girls from mining families worked underground was usually the result of parental improvidence or greed.

4. Wales

The fourth area where women worked underground was south Wales. Although this area formed part of the scandal of women working underground, the incidence was more limited than it seemed from the reports. The majority of the females who were interviewed were working in the iron foundries, which were often co-located with mines and Franks did not emphasise the distinction. He was handicapped by shortage of time and trying to cover the tardy work of sub-Commissioner Jones. The result was that much of his evidence stemmed from owners, middle-class professionals and written records rather than direct observation or discussion with workers. The Welsh language may have been a factor.

Franks was clear in his report that his figures and comments related to the mines he had visited personally. This provides only tantalising glimpse of mining in the two areas where women worked and there are no insights to suggest whether or how it was changing.

In Pembrokeshire Franks visited half a dozen pits in a small area to the north of Tenby, spoke mainly to owners and managers and had no opportunity to look at the conditions workers lived in. It is likely that his investigation lasted no more than two days. The area was part of a much older and bigger mining industry, which extended from Carmarthen Bay to St Bride's Bay and which was characterised by a number of relatively small pits. They produced anthracite, a valuable, high-quality coal.

It was alleged by some managers that mining formed part of a mixed economy and that miners were happy with shorter hours and lesser wages and supplemented their income by gardening and animal husbandry. The evidence of some pit girls reveals that miners were less happy with this situation than was being portrayed. A number of girls were from families where more than one female mined and the census recorded fifty-five-year-old Margaret Morgan and fifty-year-old Mary Herries working as colliery women at Begelly. A comment made by mine owner Captain Child was nearer the truth when he observed that women worked in the mines, and on the banks, harder than slaves in the West Indies but there was an absence of better employment in the district.

Married women as well as single ones worked, suggesting that families were too poor to allow someone to look after the home. Some families were dependent on the earning of wives and daughters because men developed serious lung disease from breathing in sharp anthracite dust.

The proportion of women working in the pits visited by Franks varied between a fifth to almost a half. Over 200 were employed in these six pits, which hints at the labour intensive nature of the work. Most were adults and there were few girls under thirteen. Their work was winding wind-lasses to haul coals from the face to the surface and adult strength was necessary.

Windlass work was almost entirely a female occupation, as men were reported not to be prepared to do such heavy work for the meagre re-muneration on offer, three or four shillings a week. A strong woman could raise 400 loads in a day. A loaded skip weighted at least twenty stones.

Women who did not work the windlasses were usually found at the surface moving and grading coal. Girls under fourteen who worked were trammers. They filled trucks underground.

The area around Merthyr Tydvill also employed female mineworkers. Franks visited the Plymouth ironworks and its attached colliery. Relatively few females worked in the mines. The main underground employment for girls was as air-door keepers, a task that was crucial for preventing gases building up. They included two six-year-olds, Mary Davis and Susan Reece. The girls had started this work at five, which was normal for this mine.

Jones visited several iron works and the collieries attached to them. His visits demonstrate that the age at which girls were employed at Plymouth colliery was extreme. At Tredegar and Dowlais air-door girls did not begin work until they were at least seven and Aberdare and Rhymney did not allow girls to work underground.

The oldest female working at a mine was eighty-year-old Margaret Morgan who cleaned coals on the bank at Penydarran colliery for one shilling a day. In the census she was listed as a pauper.

As girls got older they stopped working as air-door girls and took up roles either in the ironworks or at the pit-head. Tasks in the ironworks included wheeling coals to feed the furnaces or wheeling ashes away. These jobs were hard and Franks considered them equally as unsuitable as mining for young girls. If girls continued to work at the mine they might oil trucks to keep them in good running order.

Healthy, well-built girls in their late teens and twenties found work in strenuous surface occupations such as landing and weighing coals. They appear to have enjoyed the task. Those who did not have the strength to manage this could find a variety of work sorting or cleaning coals that had been sent to the surface. There were few roles for them underground.

*   *   *

The four regions where women worked underground in 1841 were very dissimilar in the age of the workforce, the proportion of women to men and the tasks that they performed. The reasons why women continued to work underground in some places but not others are best understood in context of the coal industry throughout the country.

There were no intrinsic similarities between east Scotland, west Lancashire, west Yorkshire and south Wales, which accounted for females working there. What linked these four areas was the absence of the factors which had brought an end to female employment underground in other areas. At certain places within these four districts, those factors were developing and affecting female employment at local level. This explains why some marked local variations existed within regions.

Women did not work in mines that had thick seams of coal as demon-strated by Newcastle and Staffordshire. When mines had received sub-stantial capital investment from owners, adolescent males, ponies and mechanisation produced a better yield of coal than employing women to move small amounts by their own efforts. Increased productivity tended to mean better wages for men, which enabled the females in mining families to remain at home instead of working. By 1841, as owners invested in existing pits or opened new ones on good seams this was accompanied by women no longer being employed underground. Yorkshire, Lancashire and Scotland all have examples of this.

In areas where alternative industries developed market forces arranged some roles into male and female occupations. The textile industry on both sides of the Pennines and product manufacture in the Don Valley and in the Midlands attracted women to them leaving mining to become a man's industry.

Sometimes the alternative employment for women was provided within the coal industry. Mines on thick seams needed a large number of people above ground to move, sort, grade and pack coal for transport. Stafford-shire and Shropshire had an established pattern of females working above ground, which may have developed from the relative lack of population in these areas and the need for someone to carry out the tasks.

The economic development of some localities where women worked underground tended to lag behind ones where they did not. Lancashire steward Joseph Hatherton offered the insight that if industry did not develop in a locality newcomers were not attracted there. Even if men preferred to keep females above ground this was not possible if they could not find boys to work with them. The females in such places had to work underground, otherwise the family would have no income. When local-ities grew and became a little more prosperous, this attracted a supply of suitable males to replace women underground and also provided alternative roles for women. In 1841, places such as Flockton, St Helens and parts of Pembrokeshire had not developed the demographic conditions that enabled mining to tip from being an industry in which family units worked together, irrespective of gender, to one in which women did not work.

In some places collective thought by miners was responsible for a decline in female labour. Where men decided that women should be excluded this could transform the workforce very quickly, although the impact might not be permanent. Tancred discovered that female labour virtually dis-appeared from the mines in west Scotland in 1837, as a result of Chartist agitation and activity, though it was beginning to re-emerge in some places by 1841. Collective thought, even if not organised activity, was occurring in parts of Yorkshire.

Several witnesses explained that women would work for less pay than men required and would accept conditions that no man would tolerate. Coal bearing in Scotland and windlass work in Wales were jobs that men refused to do. Belt and chain hurrying in Lancashire appears to have been rarely carried out by boys and they were less happy to work as drawers in very wet pits. The refusal of men to carry out certain jobs explains why women worked in backward pits, where those jobs were necessary. It was another facet of collective thinking.

The investigation by the Royal Commission produced a snapshot in time, which was fading even as the evidence was being collected. As demand grew unabated the coal-mining industry was in a period of change, but this was not recognised. Some witnesses gave information about conditions in a past that was relatively recent but which was already part of history.

Within the totality of the reports from the sub-Commissioners and the witness statements, there were opportunities for the Commissioners to have discerned some of this, but they also did not see the bigger picture. At the forefront of their minds was an emerging scandal about the moral condition of young girls who appeared to be corrupted by vice underground and turned into degenerate creatures incapable of looking after a family or a home.

The Commissioners were perhaps too focused on identifying all the examples which demonstrated the need to change working practices for females. In doing so they failed to understand the reasons why some women worked underground and who those women were. Ashley's plan to exclude all females from colliery work addressed what the Commissioners thought was the problem but it had serious repercussions for some of the adult women who were affected by it.

CHAPTER 5

All in a Day's Work
The jobs mining women carried out

I do not like the work but think I am fit for none other.

Helen Reid, 16, coal bearer

By 1841 coal mining was becoming a man's industry and the tasks performed by females were subservient ones. There were only a few isolated examples of women in roles of authority or power.

The few women who owned or leased pits inherited them. Paid agent Mr Grice managed a large, leased colliery on behalf of Sarah Palmer in Staffordshire. In Bathgate, widowed Margaret Hervie rented and ran the Armadale Inn and the small adjacent colliery of Haueauchlaw. Scottish education was vastly superior to that available in England. A woman able to read, write and do arithmetic could run a successful business and several widows in Scotland did so.

Sixteen-year-old Jane James earned six shillings a week as a coal cleaner at the Dowlais colliery. The company had sub-contracted cleaning coal on the banks to an unnamed girl who employed Jane and some men to do the work. She was one of the very few female entrepreneurs in the industry.

Preparatory work of locating viable seams of coal, sinking shafts, and planning drainage and ventilation were specialist projects, performed by engineers on a self-employed basis. This was an exclusively male profession. Women could not have gained the necessary education and experience and would not have been taken seriously even if they had the technical knowledge.

Once the mine had been sunk, a figure of authority had to make sure that it was worked in an orderly manner to avoid roof collapse and explosion and to extract the maximum amount of coal each day. Men were employed as under-stewards to control what was happening below ground and as banksmen who were responsible for the coal once it reached the surface. Larger pits also had a manager responsible for co-ordinating all the technical and business functions.

Under-stewards and banksmen were often former miners who were no longer strong enough to carry out the physical work of hewing coal. This could have tragic consequences as competence and capability were infrequently considered when giving a role of responsibility to someone whose health was damaged. In his report sub-Commissioner Symons identified that an under-steward usually earned only a fraction of the wages of a common collier and sometimes had less intelligence and activity.

In February 1842, before the Commission's report was published, young witnesses Ann and Betty Mallender and Mary Day died in an explosion of firedamp. With a sad irony these girls had spoken about God and Betty knew she would go to hell if she was not a good girl. On a winter morning, as they suffocated in the dark in a cocktail of afterdamp chemicals, hell existed on earth for them.

The inquest jury decided that their deaths were accidental but censured the under-steward, sixty-eight-year-old Martin Gomersal, who had neglected to check that the mine was free from gas before allowing workers underground. His advanced age raises the question of whether he was capable of the exertion necessary to discharge his duties properly.

✳   ✳   ✳

The main work in a mine was that of cutting coal loose and moving it to the surface. It involved a series of operations, all of which were usually sub-contracted to hewers, often known as getters, who were paid for the amount of coal that they produced. They were normally expected to produce around sixteen containers a day, the actual number depending on the capacity of the containers used by the pit.

Getting was hard, physical work. In smaller pits hewers worked in cramped conditions in restricted spaces, often lying down or crouching as they hacked and chiselled at the seams. They became hot and dirty and breathed in coal dust. Sometimes they worked up to their knees in water. Over time their health was often destroyed by the effects of bending and twisting to work in tight spaces, by the dust they had inhaled and by the water they had stood in.

Hewing coal was a job that most women and girls never aspired to. The work required stamina to be able to use heavy pit tools at the end of the working day. It also took strength to be able to wield a pick-axe with the force needed to break rocks.

Sometimes necessity intervened. Fifty-year-old Margaret Baxter began getting at Ballenerief Colliery in Bathgate around 1829 when her husband became too ill to work. Her ten-year-old daughter Mary, her son and her niece drew the coals for her in 1841. Margaret started work at four in the morning. At midday she left the children in the mine moving the coal she had cut and went home to tend to her bedridden husband. Sometimes she worked nights and had worked when pregnant until her last hour. For this she earned 2s 6d a day. Margaret was competent with domestic duties and able to pass skills on to her daughters. Mary could not sew as she was left-handed. Sister Helen made her own clothes.

There are allusions to female getters in Yorkshire and Lancashire until the 1830s. A few may have worked in 1841 but it is impossible to establish who they were or how many of them or if it was a full time role. Alice Hatherton was a drawer who sometimes got coals when the regular colliers were not in the pit. It is likely that if a woman cut coals it was for short periods only, to allow her husband to take a rest or to hasten production if there were too few coals to fill the next container when she returned from moving the previous one.

Forty-nine-year-old Rebecca Whitehead of Silkstone is an intriguing woman. The census listed Rebecca and two teenage sons as miners but her husband as an agricultural labourer. It is impossible to know whether Rebecca was acting as hurrier for her sons in order to keep her daughters out of the pit or whether she was a female getter whose sons were moving coal for her. Doctor Edwin Ellis described a female getter in this area who could earn more than her husband. She was reputed to get in an advanced state of pregnancy and on several occasions gave birth within a few hours of leaving work. Rebecca had eight children.

Symons observed fourteen-year-old Sarah Moorhouse working in a narrow passage less than 3 feet high picking down the coal with the regular pick used by the men. She was half-sitting, half-lying at her work and said she found it tired her very much. Sarah earned 1s 6d a day by getting and hurrying eight corves. This gave her a weekly wage of 9 shillings. Sarah's pay was comparable with what a man would have received for producing the same amount of coal. It demonstrates that getters could not make an adequate income by doing everything themselves.

❋   ❋   ❋

Miners' assistants had various names depending on the task they did and the place they worked. Hurriers, drawers, waggoners, trammers, putters, thrusters and thrutchers loaded coal into containers and moved them to the pit shaft from where they were hauled to the surface. Assistants could be male or female, children, adolescents or adult women. Members of the man's family were his helpers of choice as their labour was free. A miner who recruited an assistant from another family had to pay for the work. Usually the wage was paid to the assistant's father and the assistant did not know how much their effort was worth.

Conditions underground for a hurrier depended on the state of the pit they worked in and the disposition of the man they worked for. Symons observed that some getters considered the welfare of their hurriers, others ignored it and many were indifferent. Some girls reported that they were well-treated by the getter who employed them. When that man worked in the same pit as their father, this was likely to be the case.

Many hurriers were treated badly, including by members of their own family. Sometimes this amounted to no more than expecting a hurrier to do a job which was too demanding for their strength. On occasions the treatment was serious brutality. It is salutary to realise that workers rather than pit owners were responsible for some of the bad conditions that hurriers had to endure.

Elizabeth Litster, a Scottish putter, had worked for the pit master and also for the men. She said that the men drove the putters harder than the masters did and paid them less for the work. Agnes Johnston sometimes worked fifteen hour days for her father and preferred to work for the master as he only required her to work for twelve hours at a time.

By 1841 the hurriers in some pits were employed by the owner. These tended to be larger pits and assertive managers were able to control how hurriers were treated. Owners and managers who were asked about the hurriers in their pits attempted to excuse or deny their own ignorance or inaction, explaining that how assistants were treated was no concern of theirs, as getters recruited them and paid them out of their own wages. It was disingenuous reasoning which cut no ice. Symons took the view that an owner was responsible for the practises within his pit and if his orders were not obeyed dismissal should follow.

An insidious and exploitative method for getters to obtain cheap assistance was from apprentices. A few boys were indentured by parents keen for their son to enter an occupation that would ultimately provide him with a good income. Most were male orphans who were parcelled out by the parish overseers, keen to remove burdens from the poor rate. An apprentice did not earn wages for the period of his apprenticeship. The master was required to provide food, accommodation and clothes. The commission uncovered several examples of pauper apprentices living with masters' wives as callous as the masters and who provided little food, clothing or bedcovers.

Pauper apprenticeships were common in south Staffordshire, parts of west Yorkshire and Durham. Miners who did not want their womenfolk to work underground may have had no compunction in exploiting vulnerable boys to achieve this. Joseph Barker drew the wages of one getter and two hurriers who were apprenticed to him. This allowed him and his son to stop mining and his daughter to work in a mill.

Hurrying was possibly the worst job in coal mining because the work required was often too hard for the hurrier's strength and the conditions they worked in were grim and unpleasant. For boys hurrying was tolerable as it formed part of an informal apprenticeship which would ultimately result in becoming a fully-fledged getter. For females there was no progression. The only future in hurrying was the number of years they would have to slave in the role. Girls were considered to make better hurriers than boys because they were more attentive to their work and did not have to be taught how to cut coal.

By 1841 hurrying took a variety of forms. This reflected the size and condition of the pit and whether there was enough coal to justify any investment in underground roads or trucks. In some small, thin seams in the Pennines and in Monmouthshire small tubs of coal, known as corves, were pulled using a belt and chain. In others the belt and chain was needed for a few yards to drag the corve from the face to a central road where it could be pushed on rails. Belt and chain hurriers wore a broad leather belt around their waist. A metal ring was attached to the front of the belt and was fastened to a chain about 4 feet long, which ended with a strong hook. The chain passed between the legs of the hurrier and hooked on to the front of the corve. The hurrier then leaned forward and began to drag the load by walking on their hands and feet. The technique was known as 'going on all fours'. It was more efficient than hands and knees though in some of the very small passages, crawling on hands and knees was the only option. Sub-Commissioners noted that belt and chain hurriers tended scamper rather than walk and attained fast speeds. The weight they towed by this method was about twenty stones, equivalent to two adult men.

Belt and chain hurrying was a horrific practice and it appalled the sub-Commissioners who witnessed it. Symons observed several young girls harnessed like animals on his visits to thin-seamed mines at Hunshelf and Meal Hill and pulled no punches in exposing to an incredulous middle class the humiliation it heaped on them.

His first encounter was in January 1841 at Hunshelf where he was impressed with the accurate evidence given by the intelligent Harriet Morton. She was the fourteen-year-old daughter of an agricultural labourer who appeared to feel the degradation of her lot so keenly that he found it painful to take her evidence. Harriet seems to have sparked Symons' interest in identifying credible and reliable female witnesses who had a sense of propriety.

Five months later at the Meal Hill pit Symons witnessed an even greater indignity of the belt and chain when he spotted fourteen-year-old Mary Holmes padding along on her hands and feet wearing trousers which were ripped between the legs. He asked several children about this in the evening. Although Mary denied the damage to her breeches, Rachel Tinker and Ann Hinchcliffe confirmed this sometimes happened. Thirteen-year-old Ebenezer Healey left nothing to the imagination when he explained that girls' trousers were often torn between the legs with the chain. When boys were following girls with torn breeches they could see them all between the legs naked. This was perhaps the most horrific evidence Symons heard. He could only add that any sight more disgustingly indecent or revolting could scarcely be imagined than these girls at work. No brothel could beat it.

Kennedy found his own horror story at Little Bolton where the garrulous Betty Harris explained how she wore the belt and chain to drag corves up a steep passage with only a rope to hold on to and at times not even that. She complained that the belt and chain rubbed the skin off her and that it was worse when women were in the family way.

In Scotland the harnesses worn by putters went over their shoulders and they walked on their feet. Harnesses were a recent development. Franks watched coal bearers at work in pits that had not been modernised and reserved his disgust for the crail, a large basket worn on the back and flattened at the edge that fitted against the neck. It was secured by straps paced over the forehead and the bearer had to bend her waist at 90 degrees in order to wear it. He investigated in detail the barely believable workload of eleven-year-old bearer Alison Jack, who moved a ton of coal on her back each day, climbing four ladders of 18 feet each alternately with walking through passages. Franks calculated that the distance each journey covered was greater than the height of St Paul's Cathedral and she made at least twenty each day. He discovered that it frequently took two men to lift the laden crail onto the bearer's back and heard that fathers ruptured themselves doing this.

Alison and her fellow bearer Mary MacQueen carried about eight stones in weight on each journey. Mary said that her mother could carry twice this amount, the weight of two adult women. Twelve-year-old Catherine Meiklejohn carried around thirteen stones at a time. Franks thought that few men could have performed one third of her daily labour. Mary Duncan reported that some women attempted to carry over twenty stones.

The amount of strain experienced by hurriers depended on the size and weight of the container, the distance it had to be moved, the number of journeys each day and the condition of the mine floor. Longer distance did not necessarily equate to more difficult work if the underground roads were in good condition and rails had been laid. The most difficult part might be an initial few yards to get the corve from the face being worked to the rails. In some pits hurriers worked with water over the tops of their shoes, struggling with rails that were displaced by the collecting water. Getters could sometimes negotiate a premium for working in a wet pit but did not pass any of this on to the hurrier.

Typical distances for moving coal containers were up to 500 yards, which is logical considering that the pits in question were mainly on the thinner seams rather than in large collieries. Kennedy calculated that Rosa Lucas covered more than 8 miles a day moving sixteen corves.

According to her evidence, Patience Kershaw apparently covered 22 miles a day whilst thrusting eleven corves. Although this seems unlikely in an area of thin pits, Scriven went underground and formed the view that the nearest faces were 1,800 yards away and the furthest 2,000 yards. Patience's long journey may have involved a twisted and tortuous route deliberately carved out to avoid moving coal beneath particular lands above so that royalties did not have to be paid to the owner.

At Thorp's colliery in Barnsley, Ann and Elizabeth Eggley single-handedly moved corves weighing more than half a ton, which Symons described as more oppressive labour than being a galley slave. It was equivalent to pushing ten adult men. In his opinion the load was beyond the strength of any woman. The sisters pushed these trucks for about 150 yards sixteen times a day.

Some 2 miles away at the Hopwood pit Elizabeth Day's work was made more severe as she had to push a third of a ton uphill for part of her journey. The distance she covered in a day is estimated at 9 miles.

Moving corves was the most important aspect of a hurrier's work underground but it was not the only task. It was usual for hurriers to fill the corves as well as move them. There are reports of kindly getters helping girls but the prevailing picture is of getters who did nothing. Symons witnessed James Eggley, who stood watching whilst his fifteen-year-old daughter Elizabeth topped a corve by piling large blocks of coal on the top of the load to hold it in place. Symons saw her lift a lump of coal that measured 30 inches by 10 inches by 7 inches. It probably weighed 100 pounds. She lifted this more than 3 feet. It was equivalent to lifting her own bodyweight.

Coal had to be sieved before it was loaded into the corve to remove any small, worthless dust. The process was known as riddling. A riddle was 22 inches in diameter and 3 inches deep and held about 20 pounds of coal when full. It would take at least fifty turns for one of the Eggley sisters to riddle enough coal to fill their corves. Riddling was important because if a corve contained too much rubbish it would not be counted as part of the getter's output and another would have to be filled to replace it.

The amount of riddling a hurrier did depended on the number of other assistants available to the getter. Hurriers who moved heavy trucks on long runs did not have the time to fill the trucks as well and returned from their journey to collect one that had been loaded by other workers.

Hurriers were paid according to their age and males were paid more than females of the same age, even for the same work. Social conditioning and the expectations of workers were responsible for this. According to underlooker, Benjamin Miller, a twenty-year-old man would expect to receive 3s 6d for a day's hurrying whilst a girl of the same age might work for less than 2 shillings. Where a getter was hiring an assistant, it was in his interest to try and find a female as it meant that he retained more of his wage for himself.

Many girls did not know what their work was worth as they were hired out by a male relative who collected their wage. Eighteen-year-old Ann Eggley was let out by her father for 10 shillings a week. Girls in their mid teens earned around 7 shillings. At twelve they could bring in up to 4 shillings. Under ten they were worth less than 3 shillings a week. When two girls were let as a pair they would have been paid for the task and the pay split between them. A getter hiring out a daughter who was a proven hurrier to a miner in the same pit was likely to obtain a better rate for her services than an impoverished weaver trying to find a miner prepared to give his girl some work.

Working days of twelve hours or more were normal everywhere but Wales, where windlass work was too severe to be sustainable for this period of time. In Scotland Ann Hamilton often worked for twenty-four hours, had two hours rest and then returned for another shift of twelve hours. At the same mine Jane Simpson who combined pumping and putting said that she worked double, and occasionally triple, shifts. Both women said that it was their own choice to work in this manner as it gave them longer periods away from work. Janet Duncan and Mary Watson considered that shifts of twelve to fourteen hours were usual.

Lancashire mines also operated overnight when demand was good. Jane Sym worked alternate weeks of night shifts. Rosa Lucas described shifts that began at two in the afternoon and ended at three in the morning with no breaks for meals.

Hurriers were constantly on the go. They rarely had time to stop for a rest and most ate their lunch as and when they could snatch a moment. In a few pits there was a tradition of a short break being taken. Workers remained underground during any breaks as being hauled to the surface took time and would interfere with the raising of the coal trucks.

Assistants tended to work longer hours than getters, as a getter could usually cut his quota of coal in less time than it took his hurrier to load it and move it to the surface. At the end of their day getters often left the mine, whilst exhausted hurriers remained underground to finish loading and moving all the corves before their working day ended.

James Pitchforth had done this on the day the commission visited. As Scriven took Susan Pitchforth's evidence he saw her father smoking his pipe whilst Susan shivered in front of him in her torn pit-clothes. Whilst

Susan and her sister Rose continued underground, James would have left the mine and put on his top clothes before going to wait in the cabin for his daughters, who were not allowed to come out until they had moved twenty-four corves.

This lax attitude to safety in the badly run mines meant that young and inexperienced workers were left underground, unsupervised by responsible adults. It is unsurprising that tired hurriers and trappers forgot to close doors, making the mine unworkable the next day as noxious gases had seeped in.

Sometimes a collier would idle around until well into the day and then arrive to cut his coal. This meant that the hurrier, who might have been waiting at the pit for some hours, then had to work long into the evening to move all the coal. The situation was different in pits that were large enough to impose discipline about time-keeping. If managers enforced a time when all workers had to be out of the pit, getters either had to help to load the corves, or bring enough assistants to ensure that their quota for the day was received at the surface.

The strain of filling and moving corves was made worse by the bumps, scrapes, strains and bruises, which were sustained in manoeuvring heavy trucks through tight passages. Added to this was a lack of privacy for bodily functions. Witnesses were not asked about this and Susan Pitchforth probably took Scriven by surprise when she began chatting about going to any part of the pit if she needed to relieve herself and being seen by passing boys. Selina Ambler, who also raised the subject, had managed to find herself a private place.

A dreadful aspect of the work for females was the systemic brutality unleashed underground. In an age which did not shirk from physical discipline to punish those who did something wrong, hurriers were routinely subjected to violence at work without any regard being taken of their gender or age. The extent was far greater than appears from an initial reading of the evidence. When witnesses refer to being paid they are often speaking of receiving a beating, not their wages.

Punishments handed out were usually a function of a man's temper rather than a girl's misbehaviour. They often related to problems beyond a hurrier's control. Margaret Westwood was slapped for being slow because she had to wait for a turn to hook her corve to the winding gear. Betty Harris was beaten by her husband and reported that she had seen many men beating their drawer. Alison Jack had the strap from her father for not managing to complete her allotted work. Susan Pitchforth's father slapped her about the head, a dangerous practice that could lead to brain injury.

Women were regarded as the property of their husband or father and when a member of a female's family worked in the pit this person held the status of privileged punisher. Had anyone outside the family attempted to discipline a female within the family group the head of the group would have dealt with the interloper, possibly by fighting him. This right of property extended to a miner who was employing someone not related to him. Many owners turned a blind eye to what was going on. Bradford sisters, Esther and Harriet Craven, are a notable example of this.

Scriven met the girls on an early evening visit to Foster and Lassey's pit at Clewes Moor. He went underground and found Harriet crying bitterly and Esther trying to comfort her after she had been beaten and then hit on the back by a lump of coal. The rock was as big as her head and had been thrown at her by Joseph Ibbotson, the thirty-year-old getter who employed them. It was five o'clock, Harriet was about to leave work for the day and Ibbotson wanted her to continue.

It is not clear whether the girls had moved all the coal they were supposed to. Esther said that Ibbotson was lazy and sometimes did not turn up for work. It is possible that he had started work late and not cut his quota for the day. This incident was not an isolated assault. Both sisters showed Scriven the many marks of his ill treatment on their bodies. Ibbotson's mistreatment of these girls was extreme and Esther said that other men sometimes remonstrated with him for thrashing children in the pit. She also remarked that Mr Foster gave her wages to her directly as Ibbotson would try to keep some for himself if he had not worked his full hours.

The area where the Craven sisters worked stands out for the degradation of young and vulnerable girls in what were some of the most brutal conditions prevailing in the industry. Margaret Gormley was a nine-year-old thruster employed by Waterhouse's at Elland for 2s 6d a week. She moved corves for a group of getters and was regularly flogged by them, sometimes with their hands on her bottom which hurt her very much. Margaret was beaten every day and sometimes more than once a day, often by Thomas Copeland. Her evidence offers no insight as to why she subjected to this treatment. As the Gormleys' were immigrants from Ireland and the Irish were despised by other workers for their willingness to accept lower wages, Margaret's treatment begs the question of whether racism was at the root of the brutality she endured.

At the Holling Haye pit fourteen-year-old Ann Ambler, the only female working underground, was also regularly thrashed by the men who rapped her in the face and knocked her down. Ann was the only member of her family who worked at this pit.

The culture of abuse in the Lindley area may have arisen from the existence of a large number of relatively small pits whose owners had probably struggled to acquire the capital to sink the shaft, had little ready money and who needed capable colliers to bring coal out for them to sell.

Good workers were not easy to find as the better ones preferred to work in larger pits where conditions were better and earnings could be higher and more regular. Owners of small pits who were at the mercy of getters for their own income were reluctant to intervene in case a productive getter decided to leave. Esther, Harriet, Margaret and Ann worked in pits without any adult male relatives around to warn the bullies off.

Some boys in these pits also reported being viciously treated. Sam Martin, a getter at the Lister Wick pit took his misbehaving ten-year-old daughter underground to hurry for two days until she promised to be a good lass if they let her out.

Sometimes the violence underground was between workers. In Lancashire, Rosa Lucas described how Mary Tuity was beaten nearly every day with a pick handle. She had a saucy tongue and the pick was the response from men who were worsted verbally. Being readily to hand, pick handles were the instrument of choice for inflicting punishment but twelve-year-old Alice Singleton reported beatings with a pick arm, a strap and a stick. If applied with force these weapons were capable of causing serious injury.

Underground bullying took place between workers and girls, including Mary Holmes and Elizabeth Ibbetson, were hit by other hurriers. Cat fights between women sometimes broke out as they defended their turn to hook their corve on to the winding gear. Trying to take someone's turn to hook on was was as heinous a crime as trying to take the bread out of her mouth.

Women were usually on the receiving end of violence but sometimes perpetrated it. Ann Stevenson thrashed the young brother who worked with her with her hand or her foot if he did not behave himself.

Some girls denied being beaten or ill-treated underground. Managers in the better run pits were more assertive in managing the behaviour of the miners. Pits that employed hurriers directly expected getters to report misbehaviour to a steward rather than inflict punishment themselves. Some girls worked for men who were protective and treated them well. Whether a female was beaten reflected the disposition and values of the man she worked for, not her own conduct.

❊   ❊   ❊

Girls began hurrying when they were strong enough to move corves, usually when they were nine or ten. Before that age if they worked underground they were entrusted with trapping, the most badly paid but most responsible role in a mine.

Colliery owners were responsible for ventilating their pits and it was a practical necessity in pits where gas was a problem. Trapping was part of a method designed by mining engineer, John Buddles, to force fresh air to circulate underground. This prevented the build-up of the dangerous gases that could ultimately result in an explosion. Some passages were blocked by wooden doors, forcing the air to flow round the mine in a predetermined, safe manner. The drawback was that some of the boarded off passages were needed for access to and from the coal faces.

To overcome this problem a rope was fixed to the door and a trapper waited beside it in a little alcove hollowed out in the passage wall. When a corve was heard approaching the trapper pulled on the rope and opened the door. As soon as the truck was through the trapper released the tension on the rope, allowing the door to close again.

Despite its importance, trapping was regarded as light, non-productive work. It required little strength and was usually done by young children of getters who worked at the mine. The father received 6d a day from the mine owner for possibly more than twelve hours of his child's time.

The number of trappers depended on the size and layout of the underground workings. It may have been a perk for favoured getters to supply the trappers and it is possible that on occasions the getters decided whose child would take a vacant trapper position and informed the manager who was to be employed.

Eight-year-old trapper Sarah Gooder sometimes left her home at half-past-three in the morning. Trappers were amongst the first workers to enter the mine and the last to leave as they had to stay until the final corve had been dragged from the coal face by its hurrier. Most of the time they sat in the dark in their little alcoves, frightened and alone as no-one thought it necessary to give them a light. Some children became skilled at begging candle stubs that would be useless to those at the coal face. Sarah sang to keep up her spirits when she had a light but was too scared to sing when it was dark.

As mine owners and getters regarded trapping as non-productive it is unsurprising that children often did not appreciate how important a task they had been entrusted with. Trappers sometimes became bored and left their alcove. Six-year-old Susan Reece, an air-door girl at the Plymouth Mine in Merthyr Tydvil, lived very close to the mine and ran home when her lamp went out or she was very hungry. At the same pit, Franks discovered six-year-old Mary Davis fast asleep under a piece of rock near the air-door with a lamp that was spent. Jane Richards, recently promoted to road cleaner, explained that it was usual for the little ones to fall asleep when their light went out. The overseer added that when asleep they rolled off their seat and into the tram road. The fortunate ones were picked up by passing horse drivers. The unlucky ones were crushed by wagons. Broken limbs were not unusual as Mary Price testified.

Being confined to one small hole was not conducive to the health of a trapper. The only time some saw daylight other than in high summer was on Sunday. If the pit was wet they might be sitting in water all day. Pits harboured vermin, which could be very frightening for a young child. When she was woken, Mary Davis said that rats had run off with her bread and cheese. Other workers spoke of rats eating the candles.

In Wales it was not unusual for five-year-old girls to be trappers. In other areas the age was a little older. Sarah Gooder began when she was eight and Maria Mallender at nine. Girls appear to have started work at a younger age than boys as they were considered more capable of being useful at an early age. Educationalists now recognise that girls are often receptive to formal learning at a slightly younger age than boys.

Mines in Wales had tasks that were specific to the area with windlass women winding tubs of coal to the surface and pouncers working in the open air assisting to sink shafts. Whilst the work was so hard that shifts rarely exceeded ten hours, the work was not dirty as Franks commented on the clean appearance of several windlass women.

All mines had work that was individual to them. Wet pits installed pumps and employed girls such as Mary Ann Jones to operate them. Twelve-year-old Janet Murdoch also had the title of pumper but her work consisted of ladling water in a bucket and carrying it away. Widows Peggy Lowe and Madeline Adam hooked corves onto the hauling gear at the pit-cage. It speeded up the work of hurriers who did not have to wait until a hook was free. It was not a heavy or dirty job for a woman and may have been reserved for any woman the colliery felt an obligation towards. Phyllis Flockhart was involved with mine maintenance and spent up to ten hours a night underground carrying stones for the men who built the roof supports.

✳ ✳ ✳

Larger mines, and ones that produced more than one grade of coal, had a frenzy of activity at the pit-head and may have needed as many workers above ground as below it. Jobs above ground were not as well paid but there would be no shortage of applicants. Getters who were too ill to work shifts underground, women and members of the families of pit officials were all likely candidates for surface work.

Colliery officials trod a canny course when girls tried to find a job at the pit-head. Ann Eggley asked about winding work but was told that nothing was available. A pit manager's priority was to keep his getters happy. He would not upset a valued getter by giving his daughter a job that paid less than she was already earning.

Managers probably consulted the girl's father before deciding about a job above ground. Surface work for an elder daughter would be welcomed if a family had another child to take underground as it would mean an increase in family income. James Eggley was extremely attached to the 10 shillings a week which Ann earned and unlikely to agree to her moving to a role that meant giving any of this up, despite protesting that it was a shame and a disgrace for his daughters to do the jobs they did.

Older teenagers and adult women were more likely to find jobs above ground than young girls because some of the tasks demanded strength or judgement. Winding work involved raising loaded corves and also pit cages filled with people. Many pits had some form of mechanisation but the winder had to understand how to operate the equipment. They needed to be assertive to maintain safety with workers who were prepared to overload corves or hang on to ropes to get into or out of the mine faster. It was not a role for a shrinking violet.

In a small or primitive pit a girl might be employed to walk the gin horse, that drove the winding gear. Although the work was light, a young or delicate girl would lack the strength to control a frisky or frightened horse, or to make a lazy one move.

When coal arrived at the surface women were involved in sorting, grading and packing it into trucks so that it could be delivered to the buyer. This was also a job that required judgement to ensure that the customer received the right amount of coal of the correct grade. Young girls who worked on the banks were involved in the laborious tasks of moving and cleaning coal but not in the judgemental ones of whether it was suitable for sale.

*   *   *

One question posed by some sub-Commissioners, though not to mining women, was whether they were in any way ashamed of their occupation. The view of middle-class observers was that women felt not the slightest shame about their work or their pit clothes, especially when surrounded by others of the same occupation. This may have been true for girls who were from mining families but for young girls from other backgrounds the position was different. Symons thought that farm worker's daughter Harriet Morton was ashamed of the belt and chain. A similar sensitivity about hurrying can perhaps be seen in the evidence of two weavers' daughters, Anna Hoile and Esther Craven.

Although women coped well with surface jobs, working underground was exhausting and painful and in most cases demanded more than female strength could reasonably deliver without damage to health. It took place in a dirty, hidden environment and sometimes exposed women to being treated like animals.

Mining women were seen by many observers as brutish, unfeeling creatures but it would take an exceptional woman not to be stripped of some sense of dignity and self-respect by the drudgery and exhaustion of hurrying. A number of women who gave evidence to the Commission appear to have been exceptional.

CHAPTER 6

T'wixt a Rock and a Hard Place?
What choice did female miners have?

I get 5*d* a day but I had rather set cards for 5*d* a day than go in the pit.

Margaret Gormley, 9, thruster

Although it seems surprising, not all women disliked working in the mining industry. For some strong and healthy ones the hours of hard graft provided them with independence, money and freedom. As few adult women were interviewed by the sub-Commissioners it is impossible to hazard a guess at the size of this group.

Charlotte Chiles, a nineteen-year-old weigher of coals at Graig colliery, did not mind the very hard nature of her work as she had her health and strength and earned 10 shillings a week. She had left a position as a kitchen maid in a large household where she earned 70 shillings a year.

Lancashire widow Peggy Lowe, who had no family to support, hooked baskets onto the lifting winch. Benjamin Pyrah, a bailiff from Flockton, thought that girls preferred the pits to service because it gave them more liberty. A mine overseer, identified only as Z, wrote in the *Manchester Guardian* in May 1842 about a girl he found in a mine he took charge of. He gave her a job as a house servant, which she did creditably but with a constant longing to go back to her former work.

These women were independent adults and the evidence gives no hint that they had not had a free choice about what work they did. They were not employed in the worst forms of women's mining work. Charlotte worked above ground and Peggy's task was not strenuous. It is possible that the unidentified women referred to by Benjamin Pyrah and Z were working outside on the banks and not as hurriers.

Older teenagers appear to have been more independent in Scotland and Wales than in other places. At the Wemyss colliery in Fife Isabel Hugh and Janet Adamson contracted for putting on their own account which meant that they received their wages and then paid something to their families for board and lodgings. Nineteen-year-old Eliza Evans worked underground at the Aberdare colliery helping to fill trucks and boring holes, which the miner who employed her filled with explosives. She had no dependants and lodged locally.

Moving coal was the best paid job an uneducated female was likely to obtain and for women and girls who lived in mining families there was no possibility of taking other work if those who wielded authority in the family wished to maximise its income. For the majority of females, of all ages, underground work was something that they hated. Some expressed this strongly, others with a sense of resignation.

Young girls like Sarah Gooder were afraid of the dark. Older ones, aware of what could happen underground, had specific worries. Margaret Westwood admitted to being frightened after two serious accidents took place and worried about being burned. Adult women knew that years of coal-moving had damaged their health.

Females who lived with a husband or father were seen as the property of the man and few who worked underground had any choice about their work. Probably under pressure from her father, Mary Ann Hunt moved into mining in 1840 because she could not make an acceptable living from weaving when the industry hit a depression. Jane Sym married into a mining family and was compelled to become a miner when her wage as a weaver fell. The census shows that there were five males in the household, all miners, and two women.

Some miners had no scruples about their wives and daughters working underground. Banksman Joseph Gledhill thought that 22 miles a day was not too much for a girl to hurry. His daughters became hurriers at six and he was resentful that the pit owners had recently discovered two working underground and dismissed them as the work was unsuitable for girls of eight and ten. A third daughter had been dismissed at fourteen as she was considered too old to work among boys.

By 1841, a number of miners had a strong aversion to any females working underground as they thought the brutal nature of the work was something a lass should not be exposed. Several men expressed with apparent sincerity that they would not allow their wives or daughters to work underground. Women were not as quick as men to condemn hurrying as a means of making a living when it was someone else who was working underground.

At Flockton, Mary Ann Watson burst into tears at the thought of her own daughters being taken out of the pits and losing their wages. She thought that mining had not harmed her and it was not harming them. Mrs Day believed it made little difference whether girls worked in the pits or not if they had a good example shown to them at home and stated that if her two daughters did not work in the pits they would have to take a poke and go begging. Jane Wood worked underground for thirteen years and made scant effort to find something else for her daughter, Sarah, even though she acknowledged that mining was not the best job a girl could have. Jane

Margerson's mother insisted that her daughters worked as miners rather than in other occupations and Jane was taken away from service to become a hurrier.

At Silkstone, wicked stepmother and former miner Mary Fern adopted double standards. She sent stepdaughters Ruth and Ann to work down the mine but allowed her own daughter, Martha Newton, who was a similar age, to stay at home, apparently not bringing in any income.

The most callous of all mothers was Grace Craven, the mother of Esther and Harriet. She was described by Esther as a very bad mother who would not help her husband with his weaving work. Instead, Esther was hired out as a hurrier to a bullying young getter. On Esther's first morning at work, Grace followed her to the pit with a whip to make sure that she did not refuse to get into the pit cage.

Sub-Commissioners described their first descent underground as a frightening experience. A young girl, hurtling into the dark without a friend to support her must have been terrified. There is little surprise that Esther cried until she became hardened to her fate. She was in an untenable position with no one to protect her at work, at risk of being dismissed if she complained and unlikely to receive any sympathy from a mother desperate for her wage.

The mothers who made determined efforts to prevent their daughters working in a coal pit tended not to have grown up in mining families. Mary Hogg's mother was a ploughman's daughter who had kept her daughters out of the pit, saying it was not woman's work. After she died, all six girls were sent to work underground rather than in the fields. Mary considered that she was no better off mining than working on the land after the cost of tools and working clothes was deducted from her wages.

It is unclear why Rebecca Whitehead was mining, as her father and her husband appear to have been very small landowners and in 1841 her husband was working on the land. Their eldest daughters, Ann and Elizabeth, lived in as servants in different families a few miles away. The Whiteheads were not related to either family and must have made a determined effort to secure these jobs.

In Dalkeith, widowed Isabella Wilson worked underground. Her daughter Janet was a female servant and her son an apprentice shoemaker. One female miner was determined that her children learned other ways of earning a living.

The evidence of some men shows a widely held belief amongst miners that it was possible to keep a girl above ground and some were prepared to adopt a provident lifestyle to do so. Ironstone miner George Carr spoke of girls working in the pits as an abomination and considered that he had been put too as hard as any and never found it necessary to send a girl to the mine. Boys who were the sons of miners referred to sisters who stayed at home or worked in other occupations. It is not clear how far miners who said they would not allow a daughter to work underground would have gone if the alternative was starving, as none of them appear to have been in the position of not having boys who could work.

✳   ✳   ✳

Scriven and Symons collected information about income and expenditure patterns within working families. This was similar to figures mentioned by Kennedy. From these details it is possible to construct a profile of estimated weekly income and necessary expenditure for Yorkshire mining families.

A getter in full-time work earned around 26 shillings a week of which up to ten would be spent paying for hurrying and buying candles and tools to use at work. This left 16 shillings a week to maintain the family.

Rent was up to 2 shillings for a two-roomed miners' dwelling and 1 shilling a week per adult was needed for clothes and washing. Two adults could eat for around 8 shillings, with the man consuming the greater proportion of the food.

A young miner and his wife would have 4 shillings a week left over. As children were weaned the costs of food and clothes would increase by over 1 shilling a week. By the time the third child was ready for weaning the miner would need some help from the eldest child, irrespective of gender. Birth and census details indicate that Ann Eggley and Elizabeth Day began work when the third surviving child was around one year old.

The first job for very young children was trapping. The money they earned helped to offset what was being paid out to the hired hurrier and would balance the family budget either until a fourth child was weaned or until the cost of maintaining the existing children increased.

The Day family may illustrate a pattern of work for mining families. Elizabeth started work at eight and trapped for two years. She appears to have become a hurrier around the same time as Mary became a trapper, suggesting that the younger sister took over the job. Their father must have paid another youngster to work with Elizabeth, as the Hopwood pit was not suitable for very young girls hurrying alone.

In 1837, Elizabeth and Mary were working together as hurriers, though a year later Elizabeth was considered strong enough to work without help. In 1840, their eight-year-old brother, John, was working with Mary and Elizabeth was let out to hurry for another getter.

Hiring out an older teenager to work for a man she was not related to was common in Barnsley when her father had other children to help him. Ann Eggley and Ann Gooder also found themselves in this situation. This gave a significant boost to the family income.

Joseph Gooder and James Eggley were cited as miners who needed their daughters to work underground because they had no sons. These men can be traced to the census so it is possible to explore whether economic necessity was the reason why their girls remained in mining after they were fourteen.

Joseph Gooder had a wife and six children ranging from seventeen to one month. Ann and Maria were teenage hurriers let to a getter they were not related to. Fourteen-year-old Benjamin worked as a hurrier for his father and nine-year-old Sarah was a trapper. With Benjamin hurrying for Joseph a payment of 7 shillings a week to a hired hurrier would have been saved, giving the family a disposable income of 23 shillings a week. Deducting 12 shillings for rent and the parents' food and clothes left 11 shillings available to keep five children. Benjamin required good food and appropriate pit clothes, which cost 4 shillings a week, leaving 7 shillings to keep five girls. As two of them were teenagers it is likely that 10 shillings a week would have been needed to maintain a reasonable standard of living, meaning that some of the girls needed to supplement the earnings of Joseph and Benjamin.

Ann and Maria were let out as a pair of hurriers and probably earned 7 shillings a week between them, which would have covered their living costs. This brings the position of Sarah to the fore, as the family appear to have 7 shillings a week to keep two young girls and a baby, an ample amount. It is hard to believe that any financial necessity induced Joseph Gooder to leave Sarah to work in a place that scared her without providing her with a light whilst she earned around 3 shillings a week, which was probably more than her own keep.

Barnsley teacher George Armitage asserted that many a collier spent in drink the money he earned by shutting up a young child the whole week in a dark, cold corner as a trapper. It seems likely that when Sarah sat in the dark, too frightened to sing, she was working for her father's beer. At the end of her evidence Sarah asked God to bless her father and mother and sister and brother, uncles, aunts and cousins and everybody else and to bless her and make her a good servant. It is intriguing to wonder what she might have said had she known what her earnings were being used for.

James Eggley had six daughters ranging from eighteen to eleven months and a four-year-old son. A few weeks after talking to Symons, his eldest daughter, Ann, married miner John Hardcastle and moved into her own home. As Elizabeth was his hurrier James would also have had around 11 shillings a week to keep his children. Assuming that Elizabeth required 4 shillings for food and clothes this left 7 shillings to keep four children, of whom three were under five. James could not have maintained his children on 7 shillings whilst Ann was at home but the 10 shillings a week she brought in more than paid her way. The family would have had sufficient to live on had she been able to obtain winding work. James commented that it was a hard thing to lose Ann's money, no doubt brooding that her impending marriage would reduce the amount of money he had available for beer.

In her own evidence, Ann said that if she were married she would no longer work underground. It is possible that James may have tried to retain his money by letting out Elizabeth instead and taking his next daughter, twelve-year-old Martha, to hurry for him.

John Sutcliffe, the general agent for the colliery where James Eggley and Joseph Gooder worked, said that preventing girls from working underground would be hard on the Eggley and Gooder families as they depended on the work of their daughters to support their families. Whilst both men needed some help from their daughters they appear to have hoodwinked Mr Sutcliffe about how many of them needed to work underground.

Symons noted in his report that Ann Eggley and Elizabeth Day conducted themselves with much propriety and Ann Gooder could read a little. It is hard to imagine that in a town like Barnsley, where alternatives were developing, that these girls could not have found other work.

The financial details collected by sub-Commissioners indicate that it was unnecessary for every child to earn its keep unless the adults were profligate with their expenditure. For every three children a miner had, one probably needed to bring in some income. If the older children were girls, a getter would struggle to keep them away from underground work whilst they were young as he would need assistance. Until a child was strong enough to hurry alone, two children may have been needed.

How a mining family treated its girls as they grew older denoted its values. Some miners chose for their whole family to work so that they could enjoy a large disposable income. Others allowed girls to leave mining as soon as the family could manage without their work. As girls moved towards adulthood they needed to contribute to the family's income but in many cases the lesser earnings from a different job sufficed.

A fourteen-year-old hurrier could earn 6 or 7 shillings a week, wages from service were up to 2 shillings a week and 4 shillings could be earned from a factory though it depended on the girl having a skilled and responsible task. The wages girls could obtain for hurrying could be a disincentive for parents to allow them to find any other work.

In the Barnsley area some miners let out older girls as hurriers and received the money for their work from the man who employed them. In the mill towns of west Yorkshire, girls left mining when they were old enough to work twelve-hour shifts and took a job in the mills. Younger children then took their place underground. Ann Ambler, Mary Barrett, Patience Kershaw and Mary Holmes had older sisters who worked in the mills and who were paid their wages directly. It would be interesting to know how much the older girls were prepared to contribute to the household budget and how much of their earnings they kept for themselves. Benjamin Miller said that young adults were unwilling to support parents who were badly off and would move out and fend for themselves as soon as they could afford to do so.

Several witnesses were from families where girls were forced to work at a young age to help to provide a good lifestyle for adults rather than to help make ends meet. James Ibbetson could have found boys to hurry for him but thought his sisters aged eleven and eight were capital girls who were more to be depended upon. Aged nine, Selina Ambler had to go and work for her uncle because he could not find another hurrier.

The obligation to keep themselves was drummed into girls from childhood and can sometimes be heard in words they used in their statements. Mary Barrett was obliged to get a living. Her young sister, Ruth, would not stay in the pit if she could help it. In Lancashire, Betty Houghton, daughter of a pit official, was obliged to like working underground.

The money these girls earned probably exceeded their weekly keep. Mary Barrett had twelve brothers and sisters, most of them living at home. She described them as being weavers or winders or hurriers. On the census her eight-year-old brother was listed as a miner, though the occupations of Mary, Ruth and another sister were omitted.

With two adult males working as miners and two older sisters in the mill, the income of the Barrett family was likely to be around £3 a week. For a working family this level of income would have bought a good lifestyle, which was represented by adequate food, reasonable clothing and as much beer as the two adult males were able to consume.

Scriven calculated a similar level of income for the Kershaw family and Wood discovered that the Lund family also took home much more than was needed to cover their weekly outgoings.

When mining families insisted on their daughters working underground, girls would have experienced reasonable conditions at home. For girls who were not from mining families the obligation to work in a mine was sometimes imposed by social policy. Their earnings helped to provide themselves and impoverished dependants with the bare essentials of existence.

✻   ✻   ✻

Parish relief to help people who could not support themselves had existed for centuries. It had traditionally taken the form of a small weekly payment to support the person in their own home and was funded by a local rate levied for the purpose. Help had never been easy to obtain, as families were considered to have an obligation to maintain relatives who could not work. As the population grew and became concentrated in towns and as the industrialised economy ran in cycles of prosperity and downturn, there were times when large numbers of workers looked to the parish for assistance.

The cyclical nature of economic activity was not understood in the mid-nineteenth century and there was no appreciation that workers could not earn a wage if no one was prepared to hire them or that age or illness might make it impossible for someone to maintain themselves. Those without money or employment were regarded as lazy and feckless. To prevent them from becoming a burden on prudent members of the parish, the system for relief of the poor became much more draconian in 1834.

The new system came close to criminalising the inability to maintain oneself, irrespective of whether the cause was in the control of the individual or not. Obtaining outdoor relief and being allowed to remain in the family house became much more difficult other than for temporary illness or extreme old age. Those without money to support themselves had to report to a workhouse where conditions were deliberately designed to be the least desirable option available to an applicant. It was expected that people would take any employment they could find, even at a very low wage, rather than endure the harsh regime of the workhouse.

The new system of parish relief also placed the onus on relatives to support family members who could not work. Children were routinely expected to maintain parents who had no job or who were sick. In Scotland, the meagre coppers earned by a child could be the family's only income. Chronically ill Dunfermline miner John Weir had his shilling a week stopped when the poor law guardians discovered that some of his children were employed underground. Fifteen-year-old drawer Margaret Grant of Cranston kept her widowed mother who was crippled with rheumatism on 1 shilling a day. She was just one of a number of young girls who were forced into mining to support ailing parents.

With an irony that was overlooked by sanctimonious relieving officers and members of poor law boards, who complained bitterly about the degenerate character of mining girls, their decisions were the reason why some young girls went to work underground. William Jubb, owner of one of the pits at Hunshelf, explained that families applying for parish relief were told by the board to get a job for their children at Mr Jubb's or Mr Webster's coal pits; girls as well as boys. These were the pits where Symons first saw young girls harnessed like animals as they dragged coal with belts and chains.

The situation of Anna Hoile, a weaver's twelve-year-old daughter, illustrates parish relief in action and the cruel assumptions that it made. Anna started hurrying at eight when her father become too crippled to work. He applied several times for outdoor relief but the parish refused him anything as Anna's grandfather owned some houses that he rented out. The parish recommended that he should allow the family half-a-crown a week but he only gave them 2 shillings. This meant that Anna and her mother, a wool comber, had to make a living for two adults, Anna and her four-year-old sister. Anna earned 3s 6d a week which the board appears to have taken into account when deciding the amount that her grandfather should allow the family. There was no thought that Anna, the only girl in the pit, should not be expected to earn her own keep or that it was wrong for a young girl to work underground or alone with men. The sensibilities of the poor law officials were fixed on saving money, not on saving young girls.

Fanny Drake's predicament shows the reality facing impoverished rural families. Fifteen-year-old Fanny would have preferred to look after her grandmother, Widow Drake, whose terse, apparently unfeeling evidence was that she had never tried to get any other sort of work for her granddaughter. The census reveals that Martha Drake was a pauper of seventy-nine living with her son, a widower, who was trying to support three daughters on his wage as an agricultural labourer. The fact that Martha was receiving outdoor relief highlights that the family was in extreme poverty and could not manage to maintain her also. Fanny's evidence suggests that she could have been suffering occupational ill health but this would have been irrelevant to the poor law board. She received no sympathy from Symons, who thought she looked very healthy. He may have thought she was exaggerating her symptoms.

The plight of Esther and Harriet Craven demonstrates that girls could become the victims of their parents' irrational choices. Their father, Ephrahim, was a hand-loom weaver, an occupation whose members stubbornly resisted mechanisation and as a result suffered years of financial distress as they clung to their traditional methods of working. Parliamentary committees and a Royal Commission investigated their plight several times in the 1830s and finally concluded that it would be wrong to devise measures to enable a dying craft to continue. Domestic weavers unable to earn sufficient for their needs were recommended to seek employment in the mills.

It is easy to feel anger with Grace Craven for following Esther to work with a whip but Ephrahim's motivation for allowing his daughters to spend their working hours underground, being bullied by a thug, shows indifference towards them. Scriven recorded the measurements of both sisters and described one as at par and the other as under par, his term for lax, slender and feeble muscle tone. It is hard to believe that Ephrahim could not see that his daughters were not strong enough to carry out their work easily or the bruises that both sisters took home. By 1861, Ephrahim had abandoned weaving and become a joiner but perhaps he should have moved away from hand-loom weaving much earlier and earned a better wage rather than condemning his daughters to a job they hated.

❋   ❋   ❋

If a girl was allowed choice there were other occupations available in most districts and in some cases this had already resulted in females not being employed in mining. The damp climate of Lancashire was ideal for working with raw cotton and ease of transport from the docks at Liverpool meant that cotton mills proliferated in Manchester and in surrounding towns such as Oldham and Ashton-under-Lyne in the early nineteenth century. In 1841, the census recorded 62,131 women involved in cotton manufacture.

Mechanisation was slower to penetrate the woollen industry in Yorkshire as machinery tended to make threads strain and snap. Worsted, a type of long-threaded wool, proved an early exception to this problem and factory-based production developed around Bradford, providing employment for women. In the area loosely boundaried by Huddersfield, Brighouse and Halifax the thread preparation work of scribbling and carding was carried out in factories and provided work for many young adult women.

Other industries existed around some parts of the Firth of Forth. The 1841 census shows that a number of females from Tranent worked in paper mills. In the valleys of South Wales coal mining and iron foundries were co-located. Working in hot foundries was heavy and unsuitable work for women, involving heavy lifting and moving but it offered an alternative to being underground. Women in this part of Wales had a genuine choice about how they earned their living and those who worked in the mines appear to be contented with their work.

There were differences between mining and factory work and they made mining attractive to certain types of personality. Mining was less susceptible to economic downturn than factory work because the expansion of railways and the introduction of gas lighting created new markets for coal, offsetting any reduced demand from the factories and furnaces. This meant that jobs and family income were less likely to be at risk. Factory work required a discipline not associated with mining; timekeeping. Females worked in the smaller pits where getters tended to control their own hours.

Men took two, three or four days off after pay day and then worked long hours to make up the next fortnight's wages. Mining practices varied according to the demand for coal but offered opportunities for a form of work-life balance determined by the getter.

In factories, looms ran on constantly and workers had to be present throughout shifts, which often lasted more than twelve hours. There were fewer rest days and the hours could be longer than working underground. Some owners pointed out that the long hours reported by miners were usually caused by a miner taking several days off after pay day and then having to work excessively to make up his quota for the next pay day rather than being imposed on workers by the pit owners. Some daily output statistics collected by Symons suggest that this statement was accurate.

Factory work demanded attributes that were not required from hurriers who needed only the physical strength to fill and move corves. In a factory even the most menial or repetitive tasks demanded a little skill or manual dexterity and output was subject to quality control.

Despite the disadvantages that came with mechanised production, most women preferred mill work to hurrying. A few found that they were unable to work with the dust in factories and were grateful for the opportunity to work in mining.

Across the country, the most widely available employment for females was service. The 1841 census recorded 908,471 female servants. In areas where there was no industry, it was the only regular employment available. In a large house or with a middle-class professional family, domestic service offered a defined role, such as parlour maid or scullery maid or a nurse to a young child or older relative. There were others to share the work with and to talk with outside work, possibly an opportunity to find a husband from amongst the male servants. Men in specialised positions, such as coachmen or estate overseers, could maintain families on their wages. For a live-in servant the quality of even the most basic accommodation provided by a middle-class employer such as a doctor, lawyer or successful industrialist would exceed the living conditions of a girl who had grown up sharing a cramped cottage and bed with a large family. Wages were usually low as food, clothes and accommodation were provided by the employer. A girl might earn a small amount, which she could take to her family but the main advantage for a family in having a daughter who was a live-in servant was that she no longer had to be kept.

Living in was not possible for a married woman with a family. Such women may have been able to secure irregular domestic work, helping with the heaviest and least popular of household tasks.

The most usual type of domestic service was a sole general servant in a small household. Typical employers were tradesman, shopkeepers or clerics. A skilled labouring family might have a servant and it was not impossible for a mining family with several adults working. In a number of households those listed as female servants in the 1841 census were members of the extended family, sharing household duties with the wife, looking after the family of a widower, or supporting an older relative. As such, the role would have had no formal earning power beyond the provision of food, clothing and a roof over the head.

Life for a general servant depended on the whim of the master or mistress and was frequently not good. A maid of all work could be busy from daybreak until nightfall and beyond. This included lighting fires, heavy housework and laundry, washing pots and dishes, even if someone else did the cooking, and serving food. Where the employer had a business, the servant might be expected to work in the shop or workshop as well. Defined hours of work were not usual. It is likely that some domestic servants worked as hard and for longer hours in service than they would in mining.

Whatever the size of household, a servant was expected to account for how she spent any time when she was not working or sleeping. A short visit to her family each week may be allowed. Attending church on Sunday might be compulsory.

Several witnesses reported that securing a place in service was difficult for girls who were miners and Symons considered it highly probable that girls, once initiated into the moral schooling of a coal pit, did find it difficult to obtain respectable employment afterwards. Other witnesses indicated that females who had experienced the comparative freedom that existed in mining could find the restrictions placed on them by their employers irksome. It was reported that there was a shortage of domestic servants in South Wales, an area where there were opportunities for women to work at the pit-head and in manufacturing. In Scotland, Ellspee Thomson explained that the difficulty was not in finding a post but in retaining it as the liberty experienced in mining made women resentful of restraint.

Despite Symon's fears, unless a potential employer was prejudiced against mining girls, working in a pit was not a barrier to obtaining a post in service. A bigger obstacle lay with those mothers who made scant effort to educate their daughters in domestic chores. Mary Fern and Mary Ann Watson, themselves former miners, spoke of teaching their daughters some skills of household management. Mary Glover's children were covered with lice and Mary showed her breeches to boatmen on the canal for money. No matter how well presented or politely spoken she was, a girl would struggle to be accepted by any household if the person helping her to find a post was slovenly in attire, coarse in speech or behaviour or betrayed that she could not perform household tasks herself.

For mining girls who lived close to rural areas outdoor farm work could be found but it had the disadvantage of seasonality and may have only offered a few months work each year at harvest time. Witnesses in Scotland reported that it was possible to work for seven months in the fields. Seasonality would not have been a disadvantage if a family understood budgeting and could discipline itself to save so that the woman's income was not needed on a weekly basis.

Particularly in Scotland, a girl with nimble fingers could earn a few shillings making lace or sewing or knitting. In more populous areas there were opportunities making clothes, bonnets or working in a shop. The census shows that 199,222 females were employed in the manufacture of garments or accessories. Wages were low and would not provide a woman with financial independence but for women and girls who needed to supplement the family income rather than earn a large sum to make ends meet a contribution could be obtained, sometimes as a home-based worker.

A practical problem a girl from a mining family might face was learning the technical skills to produce articles to a standard suitable for selling. Formal apprenticeship may not have applied in all areas of the country or covered all levels of skill but someone may have had to be paid to teach a girl the basics of the craft. For a period the girl might not earn anything.

Whether her family were sufficiently motivated to equip a girl to earn a living outside mining might depend on how useful she was underground. Timothy Marshall described an unnamed girl who left mining to become apprenticed to his sister, a bonnet maker, after working as a hurrier destroyed her health. Agnes Grey had a deaf and dumb sister who went to Edinburgh to learn to make straw bonnets.

For women whose fingers were not sufficiently nimble to make articles for sale, there was the possibility of becoming a washerwoman. The census recorded 50,706 washerwomen, most over twenty. Carrying and heating water, washing clothes in tubs with a rubbing board and posser, drying the washing and ironing it was physically very hard work and not well paid. Five shillings a week were good earnings. Whether a woman could find customers would depend on whether people living locally could afford to pay someone to do the laundry and how many other washerwomen worked in the vicinity. Customers were more likely to be found in the towns than in the rural areas.

The 1841 census shows that women were involved in a wide range of occupations. In a number of them the woman was the wife or daughter of a man who was carrying out the work and she assisted him rather than working on her own account. Finding an opportunity in any specialised crafts or businesses was extremely unlikely for a mining girl.

For girls and women who had to earn a wage and who lived in well-populated places employment was available in factories, in service and in occupations supporting domestic consumption. The number of former mining girls who found jobs in these industries disproves the contention that they were not considered respectable enough to find alternative employment. In developed areas, the biggest barrier a girl or woman faced in obtaining or retaining a job outside mining was not her unsuitability for other work but the opposition of her family if a different job meant a reduction in family income.

✳   ✳   ✳

Sub-Commissioners considered the question of whether females working underground was necessary and concluded that it was not. They did not appreciate the differing levels of industrial development within their regions and that a few places existed within them where some females were dependent on mining for their living. Pembrokeshire, Wigan, Flockton and the upper reaches of the River Forth had very little alternative employment available.

Symons criticised the inertia of mining families in Flockton and Silkstone, who explained that girls worked as hurriers because there was nought else for them to do. He posed a rhetorical question about how other collier communities subsisted without sending their daughters underground. Flockton and Silkstone, unlike other places he visited, were made up of several small hamlets where no other industries had developed and there were few families who could afford to employ servants.

Lord Balcarras's agent, Mr Peace, advised Kennedy that there were so many females employed to the north of Wigan that it would be impossible to stop them working unless the change was phased. Franks discovered that a few medium-sized collieries in Scotland had excluded females and simultaneously improved the living standards of mining families but did not consider whether this could be replicated on a much larger scale. No sub-Commissioner identified that, in some cases, social policy rather than personal choice or family pressure forced women and girls to work underground.

By not discerning the range of factors that lead to females working underground for different reasons in different places, the sub-Commissioners inadvertently paved the way to the conclusion that a one-size-fits-all remedy could immediately eradicate one of the biggest public scandals ever to affect Victorian society.

CHAPTER 7

Non-Domestic Goddesses
How mining women managed their homes

When we come up we go and have our dinner, sometimes it is
meat and potatoes and sometimes pudding. We generally have
meat. Every day we have meat. We have water to drink.

Maria Gooder, 12, hurrier

Labouring at the pit was only one part of the life of a female miner. Away
from the mine her life was equally hard. The woman miner's own
perspective about running her home has not been well-recorded. Most
observers in 1841 thought that mining women had no ability to make a
home decent or look after a family properly. Many, though not all, middle-
class and professional witnesses such as clergy, teachers and doctors
expressed this opinion strongly.

Kennedy questioned a number of miners about the domestic skills of
women who had worked in the mines from a young age. They felt that
women who had been trained to run a home from girlhood and who did
not work outside the home as an adult had more ability to make a home
comfortable. They did not consider that women who had not known these
advantages were incapable of running a home, though they would find it
harder and might not reach the best standards. John Oldham pointed out
that even if mining women were rough and ready in their ways the same
was true of women who worked in factories. He also recognised that a
woman who worked outside the home would be attending to her domestic
chores exhausted after a hard day of heavy labouring.

The middle-classes held the poor far more responsible than they were
for the often dreadful conditions they lived in. Outside observers, who
probably employed at least one servant to help with domestic tasks, under-
estimated the problems faced by women from poorer backgrounds such as
keeping a badly-built house free from damp, getting water hot enough for
effective washing and struggling with hands that were painful and raw.

The Children's Employment Commission included detail about the conditions in miners' homes based on the first-hand observations of some
of the sub-Commissioners. Their evidence, both good and bad, is cor-
roborated by the Report of the Sanitary Commission, which visited several

areas of the country at around the same time, investigating the conditions in which workers lived.

At that time a house was little more than shelter from the elements and a place to keep a few necessities. For most workers, the concept of a house being a home had not yet developed and their possessions were scant. Some miners in regular employment lived in houses with three rooms, which demonstrates their earning power. Rent could be up to 1 shilling a week per room. Two rooms was more usual for working families. Symons measured the rooms in six miners' cottages and discovered that the smallest were about 6 feet by 4 feet. Adult heights were several inches less than they are today but conditions were very cramped in some houses.

Franks observed and recorded the poverty endemic in parts of eastern Scotland, where some families lived in squalor. Nine members of the Selkirk family squashed into a wretched, one-roomed hovel no larger than 10 feet by 14 feet. The Gordon family had scarcely any furniture in their hut and fowls were roosting over the bed. Margaret Drylie went home to a cottage with no ceiling, two dirty beds, little bed-clothing, a table, short stools and three or four broken chairs. Some families moved frequently. When asked about her lack of furniture, Isabel Wilson explained that furniture was no use as it was troublesome to flit with.

Franks also inspected the home of former coal bearer Isabel Hogg, one of the most respectable coal wives in Penston. Her rooms were all well-furnished and he pronounced the house the cleanest he had seen in East Lothian.

In Bury, Kennedy encountered the Glover family who appeared very slovenly but with Mary working all day the state of her house depended on what her mother could achieve. She was eighty-four and with failing eyesight. Mary's twelve-year-old daughter, who looked after the younger children, was handicapped.

Kennedy dismissed all the collier families at Wigan, Pemberton, Orrell, Blackrod and Aspell as degraded and wretched, with neglected, half-clothed children living in filthy dens with accumulations of excrement and filth at the doors and a savage bulldog in the house. As he also noted that Margaret Winstanley from Wigan and Jane Sym from Blackrod were clean and neat in appearance his general negativity towards miners left him insensitive to the differences that existed within areas and possibly even within households.

The horrific conditions described by Franks and Kennedy were extremes with bad homes more likely to attract comment than good ones unless these were exemplary. The Sanitary Commission visited Lancashire industrial towns. Although it found many distressing hovels it also found some mining families enjoying comfortable homes with children who were well looked after and well dressed.

Miners' wages generally held up better in times of depression than those of textile workers, enabling the prudent to avoid slums or to escape the worst effects of overcrowding. Scriven visited nine weaver's cottages. His descriptions show that in Yorkshire weavers lived in more abject poverty than miners. Kennedy found the reverse with Lancashire weavers living in more salubrious conditions than local miners. The difference may relate to Yorkshire weavers being home-based workers in a declining craft rather than to differences between mining in the two counties.

Welsh miners endured very bad accommodation. Franks discovered dilapidated cottages built on hillsides. With no attention paid to drainage, homes were prone to the effects of rain flooding down from higher ground. If the dwelling had been built in a hollow to protect it from wind the ground surrounding it could quickly turn to mud.

As pits tended to be away from built-up areas, many miners lived in cottages rather than the slums thrown up in towns to cater for the influx of factory workers. Those new to mining in any locality such as the Gormleys, who had moved from Ireland to Elland, might live in hastily erected town dwellings, walking a mile or two to work.

Sub-Commissioners in Yorkshire, Lancashire and to a lesser extent Scotland discovered some excellent accommodation provided by mine owners for their workers. At Newton-le-Willows, Mr Evans built thirty cottages each with four rooms and a small garden. There were detached privies and some pigsties about twenty yards from the houses, allowing colliers to keep pigs. Several did so. Raising and slaughtering a pig each year was a norm in some areas as meat could be preserved by salting. Crops often grew well in gardens if they were tended by a worker or his family. Potatoes were a staple but cabbages, root vegetables and soft fruits were also possible. All of this contributed to a more plentiful diet and to making the wage go further.

Kennedy found the houses at Newton-le-Willows clean, tidy and usually well-stocked with furniture. Symons considered the cottages developed by the Stansfield family at Flockton were well-furnished and kept to a good standard. In Scotland the late Earl of Mar had improved some cottages at Alloa, which were kept in a decent state by the women who had been stopped from working in the mines. Welsh mine owners were the most tardy in this respect with housing built for workers lacking drainage and an adequate number of privies.

The philanthropic owners were following the example of pioneers in the textile industry such as Richard Arkwright at Crompton, Samuel Greg at Styal and David Dale and his son-in-law Robert Owen at New Lanark. All had realised the advantages of a workforce that was stable, healthy and moral in attitudes and conduct. They had constructed basic, though good quality, accommodation for workers paying attention to ventilation, drainage and sanitation. Robert Owen drew up rules for keeping houses and streets clean. All were able to do this because their mills were in rural locations so there was enough space. The mine owners who worked to improve the living conditions of their workers also had the same advantage of needing their workers to live in rural surroundings rather than in crowded ones.

As Robert Owen recognised, the condition of a house is determined as much by the condition of the property as the attitude of the dweller. Sanitary Commission inspectors found examples of capable and motivated women demoralised by housing that could not be kept clean and habitable for reasons beyond their control. A witness spoke of a former servant who had fallen into slatternly ways. When asked why she explained that a leaking roof made it too hard to keep the home clean. When she moved to a new cottage that was in good condition her housekeeping returned to high standards.

The condition of the model houses gave lie to the assertion that mining women had no domestic skills or pride. Kennedy and Symons saw for themselves that when a mining family had decent housing to live in, a woman with motivation could create and maintain a comfortable home. Tenants were not selected according to whether the wife had domestic skills. As these houses were kept in good condition it shows that mining women who could keep house well were the rule rather than the exception. More women were blighted by external conditions than their own inability.

❋   ❋   ❋

When there was someone at home looking after the family a girl or woman returning from a day's hurrying would be able to concentrate on herself if she was not too tired. For a young girl such as Mary Butterfield, who went home part-way through the shift when her brother came to help their father, life in a caring family that drew a miner's pay would not have been harsh. Returning home she could have a wash with water her mother had fetched and heated and eat the food that had been prepared for her. If she had energy left she might be able to do some mending or knitting. For a girl who was too tired a sensible mother would balance allowing her to rest and making sure that she learned how to sew and cook.

A few motivated and clever girls used any free time to widen their knowledge. Harriet Morton worked eight-hour shifts and tried to educate herself at home. Margaret Drysdale and Alice Hatherton went to night school. Elizabeth Meek tried to teach herself to write by following her brother's copy book. Few girls reported having any hobbies or much play time. Most were too exhausted to do anything that was not necessary.

For those who had no one at home to rely on the situation was bleak. Esther Craven went home and sewed or mended clothes. As she said, she had no mother to do this for her. Dr Michael Sadler observed the greatest differences in the homes of those colliers whose wives did not go into the pits in cleanliness and good management. He believed that the female character was totally destroyed by mining. It changed their feelings and habits such that women could not discharge the duties of wives nor mothers.

A wife's lack of attention to domestic duties was reputed to be responsible for her husband going off to the pub in search of the comfort he could not find at home and for her children running around wild and unkempt. The reality was that the intense strain of hurrying meant that preparing a decent meal or responding to a needy child would be more than an exhausted woman was capable of after a twelve-hour stint. Older teenagers Rosa Lucas, Ann Eggley and Agnes Phinn spoke of barely having the energy to wash themselves when they returned home. For a woman to come home and cook a meal needed a superhuman effort.

In autumn and winter it was dark when a woman left for work. It would be dark when she returned home. It might be cold and wet. Her first chore might be drawing water from the communal pump. In some places a pump was leased to a local householder who kept it locked and charged the other families to use it. If the pump was leased the woman would have to fetch the key to unlock it, draw water and then return the key, all adding to the effort required.

If the house had been empty all day she would have to light a fire to boil water for washing and cooking. If there was not much water available, or she was too tired, having a wash might become a quick wipe of the face and hands with a dampened rag.

Getting a meal together would be difficult. Menus were restricted less by money than by storage. The Sanitary Commission found that workers' houses were prone to damp and lacked effective ventilation. Many food-stuffs went bad very quickly, especially in warm weather. If a wife was out at work all day, putting meat on the table that evening was very difficult. The most likely meal would be boiled potatoes or porridge, foods that did not go off too quickly.

Helping a wife with the domestic tasks necessary to get a meal onto the table was not seen as man's work, even if both had been out at the pit all day. In Lancashire, where a man's drawer was often a young adult woman, there were reports that she joined him at the pub and helped to drink the earnings. For couples without children it was a practical response to circumstances. Food could be obtained in some pubs. Some workers chose to drink beer rather than eat much. It provided some calories, might temporarily stave off hunger and could create a short-term feeling of well-being, offsetting the harshness of working for many hours in dusty and cramped conditions.

This may not have happened widely. Census returns suggest that the number of women who worked as miners all day and were solely responsible for running a home was not great. Many lived in a household where there was another woman who remained at home, apparently keeping house. When extended families lived close together it is possible that childless couples had something to eat with one of their parents before heading off to the pub.

If, as reputed, Lancashire miners sought out girls who worked in the mills because of their superior domestic skills it is hard to believe that the women lost them as soon as they got married. That they went to the pub with their husband suggests that the daily work cycle and living with extended families meant that some young women had few opportunities to put their domestic talents to use. If they did not use their skills regularly a reduction of ability might turn some women into the struggling creatures that some witnesses complained about when it became their turn to take on the running of the house.

Mining women and girls in all areas spoke of being able to cook, sew, knit or mend. Agnes Cook made her own clothes and stockings. Mary Hunter's grandmother taught her to knit stockings for the family. Ann Fern had to stay at home on Sundays to learn jobs around the house. Bessy Bailey had to stay at home to help her father to get the dinner ready and to wash the pots up.

Older girls were involved in helping with younger children and in nursing sick relatives. Esther Craven's distaste for nursing may have arisen from having to look after her dying mother.

Once women started working outside the cottage economy they could not fit in everything necessary to run a house in the reduced amount of time available. Service industries and retailers developed to produce and supply goods that women did not have the time or skills to make but these could swallow up a substantial portion of the family wage as a one-off outlay. A tailor charged Hannah Bowen 2s 6d to make her working outfit. This was almost a week's pay. The cloth cost her a further 4 shillings.

Some witnesses unkindly commented on the inability of mining women to cut a shirt or make their own clothes. The large number of tailors and dressmakers recorded in the 1841 census suggest that middle-class women would also have struggled to do this. The standards middle-class witnesses expected of mining women were probably higher than their own wives and daughters could have achieved doing the same tasks.

✳   ✳   ✳

Running a home in the early nineteenth century was laborious and made harder by the fact that some women were pregnant for a large proportion of their fertile years. Insanitary living conditions led to diseases and in large families, or when houses were crammed together, it is likely that someone was unwell much of the time. When women stopped producing children they may have needed to take in and nurse an invalid relative. Providing care to vulnerable family members was a hidden additional role for many women.

The daily round of tasks was bleak and unending. A woman had to keep the house clean and tidy. Excrement had to be disposed of, preferably at the nearest cess pit. Water needed drawing from the nearest pump and carrying back to the house. It had to be boiled for family members to wash themselves when they came home from work. Washing clothes was miserable outside work with the washing and wringing having to be done by hand on a day when the washing might dry. Yet the clean and whole-some appearance of colliery girls outside work indicates that mothers must have been carrying out this work properly. If Esther Day was not looking after her family properly it would have been impossible for her daughters to be interviewed by Symons looking clean, decent and respectable only a few hours after one had scandalised him by working underground stripped to the waist. Clothes worn underground wore out quickly so mending was another regular task, either to extend their life or make them suitable for a smaller child. Some women made some of the family's clothes.

Symon's visit to the six mining cottages showed that an industrious and provident mining family could generate a comfortable standard of living, which was reflected in the appearance of the house and in the number and quality of possessions. Most of these cottages had beds and bedding in good condition, enough tables, chairs and storage for the family, a clock, fire irons, crockery and an impressive collection of bibles, testaments and other religious books. These had been supplied to the children by the Stansfield family. To Symons' consternation the air and light in Anne Charlesworth's cottage was impeded by her husband's six larks, which were in cages in the window. He was impressed by the good influence that dressmaker Martha Taylor had on her home and on her husband. Jane Wood was commended for her curtained windows. As she had worked in the pits for thirteen years, starting when she was seven, her cottage disproves the view that girls who became miners at a young age made bad wives and mothers.

Mining families were distinguished from other workers by their food. Where there was someone at home to prepare meals their diet was not unhealthy. The regular consumption of meat, and to a lesser extent cheese, made their diet superior to that of other workers.

Some middle-class observers considered that women who left the pits when they married were unable to manage money and spent improvidently. Witnesses to the Sanitary Commission condemned workers for buying chops and steaks that were much more expensive proportionately than joints of meat, but not necessarily so if the joint went bad and some of the meat had to be thrown away. Many houses lacked proper storage so working families were obliged to shop little and often. Local provision merchants sold basic foods in small quantities to cater for this. Shopkeepers bought sacks of foods and then weighed them out and sold them in plain packets. Over the next decades this method of retailing small quantities developed into the branded packet food industry as housewives strove to overcome one of the major hazards of buying food, adulteration.

It was common practice for shopkeepers to mix food with other substances to maximise their own profits. At best adulterated food was of inferior quality. At worst it could either have been laced with something poisonous or mixed with something to disguise that it had gone off.

Cheap food could be false economy. Miners needed a good diet to maintain the strength to hew coal. If a worker had to stay at home with vomiting and diarrhoea the family would have no income for a few days. A general storekeeper serving the pit community at Worsbrough Dale stocked only the best articles, otherwise he risked not being able to sell his wares. Miners' wives chose to buy butter at 1s 2d a pound rather than another type that was tuppence cheaper. Butter was adulterated by putting extra water and salt into the churn. It was not harmful but the resulting product was less enjoyable to eat.

Cooking equipment and space was also pertinent in choosing purchases. Food was usually cooked by boiling it in a tin kettle suspended over the fire or roasted or stewed in a primitive oven placed above or alongside it. Some families owned a backstone for baking oatbread. Cooking a large joint or a tougher cut of meat took longer and used more fuel than a small, tender one and mining families had to buy coal. Evaporating water added to any problems of damp within the house. Kettles over fires were dangerous, especially in a small room on a wet day where a handful of young children might be playing giddily. Locality reports from sub-Commissioners referred to children who had died at home from burns and scalds.

...ners' houses at Elsecar, near Barnsley, erected by the Earl of Fitzwilliam in the early 1830s. *(Brian Elliott)*

...Huskar Memorial, All Saints' churchyard, Silkstone. ...ven girls and fifteen boys died in a freak accident ...r here in July 1838. *(Denise Bates)*

Detail from the Huskar monument showing the names and ages (8–17) of the girls and young women killed. *(Brian Elliott)*

Remains of a pit at Hunshelf, near Stocksbridge. Seven girls hurried wearing the belt and chain at pits in this area in 1841. *(Denise Bates)*

Anthony Ashley-Cooper, 7th Earl of Shaftsbury (1801–1885). *(Brian Elliott collection)*

A rare photograph of a Commission witness, Harriet Craven (second right) in old age. *(Patricia Blocki)*

	REGISTRATION DISTRICT				ECCLESFIELD			
1842 DEATH in the Sub-district of	Barnsley				in the	County of York		

Columns:–	1	2	3	4	5	6	7	8	9
	When and where died	Name and surname	Sex	Age	Occupation	Cause of death	Signature, description and residence of informant	When registered	Signature of registrar
298	Twenty second February 1842 Barnsley	Elizabeth Mallender	Female	14 Years	Daughter of Joseph Mallender coal miner Beleverley	Accidentally burnt by the explosion of fire damp	Thos Lee Coroner Wakefield	Twenty fourth February 1842	Jno Oxcliffe Registrar

	REGISTRATION DISTRICT				OF WORTLEY			
1875 DEATH in the Sub-district of	Penistone				in the	County of York		

Columns:–	1	2	3	4	5	6	7	8	9
No.	When and where died	Name and surname	Sex	Age	Occupation	Cause of death	Signature, description and residence of informant	When registered	Signature of registrar
27	Sixteenth November 1875 Hoylandswaine	Rebecca Whitehead	Female	82 Years	Widow of Daniel Whitehead a Farm Labourer	Spasms 1 month old age; certified by Chas Cod Rowley M.R.C.S.	The mark of Elizabeth Lockwood, niece present at the death Hoylandswaine	Sixteenth November 1875	Hugh Milly Registrar

ath certificates of Commission witness Elizabeth Mallender who died underground in 1842 and former
ner Rebecca Whitehead who died of old age in 1873.

e London home of sub-Commissioner Jelinger Symons where he lived in 1841. (*Denise Bates*)

Woodcut of a coal bearer. This 1842 image in the Royal Commission report illustrated the horrible and obscene toil of many women. (*Ian Winstanley, Picks Publishing and Coal Mining History Resource Centre*)

Women coal bearers in Scotland.
(*Brian Elliott collection*)

Putter in Midlothian. This image in the 1842 Royal Commission Report shows that female workers did not always wear trousers. (*Ian Winstanley, Picks Publishing and Coal Mining History Resource Centre.*)

...rgaret Hipps, age seventeen, coal putter, as ...trayed in the Scottish Mining Museum. (*Brian Elliott*)

Sarah Gooder, trapper, waiting in her alcove. (*Margaret Bates*)

...n Ambler and Will Dyson being hauled out of the pit, the most controversial image in the 1842 Royal ...mmission report. (*Ian Winstanley, Picks Publishing and Coal Mining History Resource Centre*)

Harnessed hurrier. Regarded in 1842 as a ba[...] breasted female, the rest [...] the hurrier is masculine i[...] appearance. (*Ian Winstanley, Picks Publishing and Coal Mini[...] History Resource Centre*)

Another shocking image from the 1842 Report: a young women and a boy miner pull and push a fu[...] tub of coal along an underground roadway. (*Brian Elliott collection/ Wharncliffe Publishing*)

A view from Meal Hill near Wooldale shows the nature of the Pennines where numerous small pits were worked. The undeveloped nature of the surroundings shows that there were few alternative ways of earnin[...] a living in these remote areas. (*Denise Bates*)

n Gooder pushing one of the biggest trucks in the
ghbourhood at Thorp's Colliery, near Barnsley.
garet Bates)

Lacking moral decency? Men who considered
themselves upstanding citizens spoke of watching
immodest colliery girls washing themselves outside
their cottages. (*Margaret Bates*)

herine and Hannah Thompson draw coals for their father. (*Margaret Bates*)

Margaret Drysdale drawing a coal cart; former coal bearers push coal trucks in a newly -modernised pit. (*Margaret Bates*)

Women carrying baskets of coal, Dowlais, South Wales, 1875. (*Brian Elliott collection*)

Two pit-brow women empty a tub of coal on the tipler, probably at a Wigan pit, c.1890. (*Brian Elliott collection*)

Until 1831, miners in some areas were paid in tokens, which they exchanged for goods at a shop run by the mine owner. The goods were usually overpriced and of dubious quality. Other than in parts of Wales and Staffordshire, where some owners continued to operate tommy shops illegally, if miners wives paid high prices for their food it was by choice and they obtained value for their money.

Meals were based around a few staple foods available at the time and women had no understanding of nutritional value. They knew what the family needed to eat but not why. Had the available foods not happened to contain protein and carbohydrate it is debatable whether mining would have been the feasible occupation that it was. In Scotland where eating meat was rare Franks noted that a miner's diet was insufficient in quantity and too poor in quality to sustain severe labour.

Breakfast was often porridge, which would be warm, filling and con-sisted of carbohydrate, which would provide energy. Girls working at the mine reported having some bread for lunch and occasionally cheese. The bread was a cake made from oats. They may not have had anything to drink at work unless they had something to carry liquid. Underground water was often avoided as it could be contaminated.

The evening meal consisted of potatoes which were filling. If families grew vegetables these added variety. Many witnesses reported eating meat, at least on some days. Mutton and bacon were eaten regularly. Pigs were relatively easy to raise. The terrains where mining took place were usually not in areas of good farmland and sheep were easier for small-holders to rear and bring to the local market than cattle.

Meals were usually accompanied by tea or coffee though some families brewed their own beer. As tea and coffee were made with boiling water this killed contaminants.

Working miners ate good food and this extended to any women and girls working underground in strenuous roles. Whether they all got enough calories from their diet to sustain the amount of physical activity is debatable. Many of the girls were adolescent and calories were needed to fuel growth, as well as provide the energy to move loaded corves. Pregnant hurriers needed extra calories to support the pregnancy. Jane Sym felt hungry on occasions even though she lived in a family with five men working as miners. Her husband was a drunkard, which suggests that in the spending choice between sufficient food and sufficient drink, beer was winning.

Women who did not mine needed fewer calories. Flockton miner's wife Margaret Child did not eat any breakfast. Her neighbour Nancy Metcalf drank tea instead of eating dinner. Jonathan Clayton's mother sometimes went without food to allow him to have plenty to eat.

As their family increased in size, many women limited their own food intake to make the money go further. Reducing her own food consumption to a minimum may have been an economy practised by mothers who wanted to keep their girls away from the pit.

The diet of girls from non-mining families would not have been as good as those from mining ones as their wages were needed to provide basic essentials for the family. A similar situation existed in Scotland for the girls who worked to support their ailing parents. Franks described fifteen-year-old Margaret Grant, the sole support of her sick and widowed mother, as having all the appearance of one worn down by hard work and want of food.

Organising food for the family meant an early start for a woman preparing a breakfast of porridge and tea and getting some bread and perhaps cheese together for those who were going out to work. When the workers returned more than twelve hours later the woman would have to cook a hot meal, clear up and supervise the bedtime routine of youngsters.

The need for a woman to burn the candle at both ends was not understood by Commission witnesses who held mixed views about women appearing to have some leisure time. In Barnsley it was said that colliers' wives lived ladies' lives but it did not raise eyebrows. A rent collector in Lancashire was scandalised to find miners' wives sitting together enjoying a cup of tea. Even if a woman had some spare time during the day she started her chores earlier and finished them later than her husband whose remit was to relax when he returned from work.

✳   ✳   ✳

When the day's work was finished a woman had to contend with difficult sleeping arrangements. Anyone working in a mine would need a good night's sleep but they may not have got one. If a family lived in a three-roomed house, two of the rooms would be given over to sleeping accommodation and there might also be a mattress in the living area.

The Sanitary Commission studied households in Lancashire, the area where Mary Glover lived. They discovered numerous instances of overcrowded dwellings and beds being shared by three, four and occasionally five people.

Mary and her husband lived in a household of ten. They shared with her parents who were in their eighties, her father-in-law who was sixty and five children aged between fourteen and three. How these people arranged themselves for sleeping can only be hypothesised but it is likely that each couple shared their beds with either two or three children. The father-in-law may have had a mattress in the living room. In large households, night shifts could have been an advantage. There would have been more room to turn over in bed.

At Falkirk seventeen-year-old Ann Hamilton's family had three beds in two rooms. Three boys slept with their uncle in the kitchen. In a small adjoining bed were three teenage girls. In the other room the parents slept with three children in a moderate-sized bed. The other houses in the vicinity were equally overcrowded. Margaret Grant and her bedridden mother lodged in a three-roomed house occupied by twenty-one grown people. Ten slept in one small room.

The Sanitary Commission noted that families tended to put all the children in one room and parents kept the other for themselves. When it was no longer feasible to have all the children in the same room the older daughters would move in with the parents.

In a family of six children it is likely that the Eggley sisters were sharing their bed with at least two younger sisters. Whether Ann and Elizabeth got enough sleep with younger children wriggling around is unlikely. Elizabeth said that she had often been obliged to stop in bed on Sundays to rest herself.

For large families making enough space to sleep well would be difficult. How they managed when not asleep was even more challenging. In rural areas overcrowded cottages could spill children out to run in the fresh air if the weather was fit. In back-to-back town slums even the space outside was restricted. When families were like the Glovers or the Amblers with five adults and several children conditions on a wet day can only be imagined, especially if adults had volatile temperaments. There is little wonder the pub proved so attractive.

Babies bawling, children playing, mother trying to cook, exhausted hurrier trying to rest, men tipsy after a visit to the pub, older relative needing nursing, the smell of coal dust inside, the smell from sewerage outside, rain teeming through a hole in the roof or flowing under the door all add up to a very trying life. Little wonder the vicar calling on pastoral duties, the teacher trying to interest the family in sending their children to school, or the doctor reluctantly entering the house to certify a death formed a negative impression of the capabilities of mining women. What differentiated the astute witnesses from the sanctimonious was the under-standing that some women were maintaining their homes and families as well as anyone could have done in difficult circumstances over which they had no effective control.

CHAPTER 8

Not In My Back Yard
Religion, education and health

I have been hurt but colliers don't make any account of being hurt
unless their bones are broken.

Margaret Winstanley, 24, drawer

Ascertaining the moral condition of mining children was a key element
of the sub-Commissioners' investigations. In their own eyes, upper and
middle-class Victorians lived by a strong moral code. They measured
moral standing by outward appearances such as going to church, reading
the bible, being clean and respectably dressed, not using profane language,
not getting drunk and not having illegitimate children.

For some, morality went further and condemned the lifestyles of the
poor. There was little notion that the condition of the poor might be the
result of the decisions of the better-off. Few felt any responsibility for
improving the lot of local families struggling in bad conditions not too
many miles away. There were some exceptions, such as the Stansfield
family, who made an effort to improve the lives of their workers but many
better-off people with a conscience were more interested in the efforts of
missionaries taking Christianity to far-off parts.

Moral condition was an ill-defined concept and the better-off confused
morality with income and wealth. The able-bodied poor were considered
to be making the wrong moral choices. They did not attend church, got
drunk, produced illegitimate children and applied for parish relief.

Many Victorians had not realised that the poor were wholly dependent
on what their employers would pay them and never considered whether
this was enough to cover a family's necessary living costs. The poor relief
system introduced in 1834 thought that the able-bodied should be prepared to work longer and harder to earn the additional coppers they
needed and that young children should contribute to the family income.
That the human body was not capable of the hours and intensity of labour
that social policy advocated was never considered. Wages were regulated by economic laws, not humanitarian impulses.

The hymn *All Things Bright and Beautiful* was composed in 1848. The now
omitted verse:

The rich man in his castle
The poor man by his gate
God made them high and lowly
He ordered their estate

summed up a prevailing view that inequality was ordained by God. It was comforting for the better-off to believe that the poor were responsible for their squalid lifestyles. If the poor changed their ways, worked hard, spent wisely, attended church and behaved as instructed by the bible they might become sober, industrious, contented people bringing up their children in good ways, accepting of their poverty and station in life.

Helping the poor to understand the failings of their moral choices and giving them ways to do something about it fitted in with the missionary zeal for converting the heathen. Two things were considered necessary: a bible and the ability to read it. Someone who could read could study the bible and the prayer-book, read hymn sheets in church and generally become a better person.

Mining families in 1841 were regarded as ungodly. The evidence of the children showed that not many attended worship regularly. In this they differed little from other workers in towns. Church attendance had declined in earlier decades as people left their home villages in search of work in factories. Freed from the expectation of the family and the watchful eye of the local clergy those who did not want to be cooped up in church found it easy to stay away. Some mining girls had never been to church, Sunday school or been taught by their parents anything about God or how to pray. Yet baptism dates for some of those girls can be found in parish registers, showing that the pull of the church had not been broken, even if miners understood little about what its services and ceremonies meant.

Attending church was a symbol of middle-class respectability made possible by money that could buy help with housework. Married women miners seldom went to church. Betty Harris explained that unless they had someone running the home for them mining women spent Sundays doing whatever domestic chores could be fitted in. Unmarried hurriers who had been out the night before might be sleeping off the effect of the alcohol they were reported to consume.

Others might be trying to recover their strength after six days exhausting work. There had been a long tradition of St Monday, when workers took Monday off as well as Sunday. This was dying out in the mid-nineteenth century with factories requiring workers to be present six mornings a week. Some mine owners followed suit. Faced with a choice between relaxing on Sundays or going to church most miners elected to rest. Joseph Charlesworth, who smoked and attended to his cages of larks at the expense of his religious duties, incurred the wrath of Symons.

A different issue was the location of churches relative to where mining families lived. A number of churches were built and consecrated in the 1850s because communities had sprung up in previously unoccupied areas. Ann Eggley lived too far from any church to attend though she acknowledged that she preferred to walk in the open air on Sundays.

Some people attended two services a day. With conspicuous church attendance came the concept of dressing up in Sunday best, another outward expression of a good moral lifestyle. It created another barrier for the very poor. Esther Craven had no clothes fit to go to Sunday school in. Jane Kerr and Esther Peacock had no clothes for kirk. Wood noted that the standard of mining children's clothing was better in the more middle-class areas. He linked this to the need to be appropriately dressed for Sunday school.

Mining families who wanted to go to a religious service had to contend with an array of options. The nineteenth century was a time of zealous debate amongst Christians about the route to salvation. The Church of England had a large number of parish churches, though these were in older centres of population. Seats in some churches reflected the local social hierarchy with pews reserved for important families, leaving workers to stand at the back.

Catholicism was no longer seen as a dangerous religion and gained impetus with the influx of immigrants from Ireland. In Scotland, Presbyterianism had been popular for more than a century. In Wales nonconformism was strong. Dissenting sects had become established in England though not uniformly. Methodists, Wesleyans, Baptists, Congregationalists and Quakers had chapels and meeting places that were often patronised by the new industrial class. They set up Sunday schools to attract adults through their children. Scriven thought that many were interested only in the numbers that they could claim adhered to their interpretation of the truth and enticed them to their Sunday schools by secular activities such as parties and jubilees.

Much of the debate about doctrine went over the heads of the uneducated classes. Those who attended a religious service may have chosen the nearest place, or to conform with others in the area, or a place where their children attended Sunday school or simply a time that suited them best. With a choice of church and chapel a short distance from her home, Elizabeth Day went to a Methodist service on Sunday evening. The Stansfields made it compulsory for children working in their mines to go to the local church after Sunday school unless their parents took them to another religious establishment.

Not many mining girls appear to have attended any form of worship as a family or to be strongly religious. Margaret Saville went to the Methodist chapel with her father and mother. Ann Francis attended the Alloa Episcopal Church regularly. Only thirteen-year-old Margaret Brown was described as religious.

One effect of the scramble for souls was in some popularisation of practises within worship. Churches wanting to attract attendance increasingly used services that included music as well as sermons and ceremonial. Charles and John Wesley had composed *Love Divine*, *Oh For a Thousand Tongues to Sing* and *Come Thou Long Expected Jesus*. Hymns had been set to music written by Bach and Handel.

※　　※　　※

More mining girls attended Sunday school than church or chapel. For parents, getting children from under their feet for a couple of hours would be attractive and they were probably not too concerned about what instruction their children received. Some Sunday schools in England attempted to teach reading and writing. This was to enable the pupils to read the bible and other religious books. In Scotland they concentrated on religion. A system of primary education had been established for almost two centuries covering other aspects of learning.

Teachers stressed what would happen to children when they died depending on whether they were good or bad. Many must have spent sleepless nights after hearing descriptions of the fires of hell. Emma Richardson knew that hell was a burning place. On her first day at Sunday school Anna Hoile discovered that if she were bad she would have to be burned in brimstone and fire. It would be interesting to know whether any girls ever imagined similarity between hell and a coal mine. Some of the sub-Commissioners did.

Studying scripture often meant learning the catechism or bible verses by rote. Some girls could repeat the Lord's Prayer but without understanding. Eleven-year-old Betty Mallender failed to explain the meaning of trespass. Hannah Vaux answered fluently that Jesus Christ came to save us from sin and was reviled by men, nailed to the cross and rose again. She was not asked to explain what this meant.

Despite lessons in Sunday school or church several girls did not understand what they had been taught. Mary Day had heard of Jesus Christ but not taken a deal of notice. Sister Elizabeth though he was Adam's son. Emily Patterson did not know whose son Christ was. Elizabeth Lawrence, Mary Price and Harriet Thorpe had never heard of him at all.

Regarding these girls as ignorant misses the point that teaching methods and quality of teaching are important in transmitting knowledge. Clergymen with masters degrees were not necessarily able to convey information in terms that uneducated children would understand, remember and explain. Lay people trying to teach may have lacked teaching skills or underpinning knowledge of their subject. The girls who displayed good understanding of the scriptures were probably highly intelligent.

In the early nineteenth century education was not compulsory though it became more widespread in the 1830s. The Factory Act of 1833 had been innovative in requiring factory owners to provide two hours of education each day for the children they employed. This was intended to help children who spent their days in factories to obtain some religious knowledge. The law was often disregarded but it set a marker. Some of the large mine owners established schools for the children of their miners but not all families took up places. The Stansfields organised evening sessions for brighter children. Most employers took no interest in whether a mining family educated its children or not. Some considered that children could obtain education by going to school after work but, in reality, few exhausted girls would be alert enough to learn.

Kennedy identified from Sunday school records that twice as many children under thirteen could write their name than thirteen to eighteen-year-olds. Younger girls tended to report going or having been to school. Older teenagers often had not, indicating that education was becoming more common. The compulsory registration of births, marriages and deaths, which began in 1837, would have brought some families in contact with a practical use for reading and writing for the first time, perhaps stimulating interest in a child trying to learn.

Religious establishments provided secular education. Many day schools were linked either to the Church of England or to noncomformism. If girls went to school it was probably to either the nearest or the cheapest unless a parent had a strong doctrinal preference or had been upset by a teacher. Catherine Thompson was taken out of school by her father after being made partially deaf by a caning across the head when she was six.

A few schools offered a mechanical curriculum and some dame schools existed for young children, which were a mixture of child-minding and basic reading. For mothers who needed somewhere to leave young children whilst they worked the quality of the teaching by the women who ran them was not likely to be a priority.

Some sub-Commissioners made determined efforts to ascertain the quality of education provided by local schools and whether a child could read and write. Symons took a particular interest in this to the extent that he was able to categorise individual establishments. Wood dismissed educational standards as very poor, except in the night schools.

The quality of learning varied greatly. Welsh education had been found to be very backward in mining areas in a separate investigation into education in Wales in 1839. Eliza Lewis who read English and Welsh, wrote a little and had tolerable scriptural knowledge was a notable exception. In Scotland even amongst very poor families a number of girls were literate. Franks added comments at the end of the girl's evidence and discovered about twenty very talented lassies.

Twelve-year-old pumper Janet Murdoch read and wrote remarkably well. Margaret Jack had an excellent knowledge of scripture history, was fairly acquainted with geography and had a very good knowledge of multiplication. Despite adverse family circumstances, Ann Hamilton read and wrote very well and was very well informed. Margaret Grant was a very intelligent lassie. Elizabeth Litster read and wrote very well and was clever and ready in her replies. Symons discovered competent readers, Harriet Morton and Ann Hague, at the same pit. In Lancashire Alice Hatherton could read and was learning to write. She attended night school three times a week. Wood interviewed thirteen-year-old John Walker who had been taught to read by his mother. Had these girls been born into different social circumstances, it is intriguing to wonder what alternative legacy they might have left for history to study.

The barriers to a mining girl receiving education were not confined to the lack of obligation of mine owners to provide it. Wood identified that most parents were keen for their children to learn but did not go out of their way to make it possible. The end benefit for the family was too ill-defined and if money was tight the coppers spent on education would be an early economy. When a girl's work was needed at the pit, learning could only continue at night if she was not too tired and there was a convenient school. Jane Kerr had no school near enough to go to.

Some continued to attend Sunday school after they started working. Unless a girl was particularly bright or motivated this was unlikely to be sufficient to develop or maintain any proficiency.

Many girls stopped attending any school when they started work and soon lost what knowledge they had gained. Whether a girl retained what she had learned depended on how ingrained the skill had become by the time she left education. Eight-year-old Janet Allen had been able to read but lost the ability within nine months of starting work.

A few girls did manage to hold on to and develop their learning. Fourteen-year-old Agnes Reid read the *Weekly Dispatch*, which was lent to her father, and sometimes *Chambers Journal*, and surprised Franks with her general knowledge.

Statistics produced by the sub-Commissioners confirm assertions that greater effort was made by parents to educate boys than girls with higher proportions of boys generally being identified as being able to read. In Lancashire, three times as many boys could write their name, though at

8.4 per cent this was not a large number. Symons' analysis of school attendance shows that far more boys were sent to school than girls.

When they had to pay a few pence a week for every child who went to school, those with large families may have decided that it was better value to try to educate a boy who might then be able to better himself and his family rather than a girl whose destiny was either marriage or a spinsterhood helping to look after the family. As schools did little to prepare a girl to keep a house, some mothers may have preferred to keep them at home to teach them domestic skills.

Not all families took the view that educating girls was unimportant. From the number of mining girls who reported having attended school before they started work, parents were not averse to allowing their girls to try to learn. Ann, Maria and Sarah Gooder all learned to read. Elizabeth Eggley attended school four times but stopped as she was unable to get anything to go in. Her father's grasping attitude to money may have been the reason, if he could not see any immediate benefit from the expense.

Timothy Marshall reported anecdotally about two families, one earning 24 shillings a week that refused to send its children to school and one earning 14 shillings that did so. The values of mining families were split in this period between the immediacy of good living and a more aspirational outlook.

In some schools fees were charged according to what subjects the child was taught with writing costing extra. This is one reason why those who could write were fewer than those who were learning their letters. Scriven found that only seven percent of children could write their name though fourteen percent could read an easy book.

Some of the readers coped either by spelling out the letters or by remembering words, but were unable to understand what they read. Some confused reading with learning by heart. This is not surprising when the purpose of reading was focused exclusively on a small number of religious texts. Elizabeth Brown read the Testament, apparently the chapters she had already mastered. She struggled to read part of the instructions provided by Franks even though they were in much larger print.

Sub-Commissioners checked claims that children could read and write. They were tested with individual letters, words or easy reading books. The few who read fluently progressed to religious texts. Those who said they could write were asked to write their name. Those who knew numbers were asked simple sums. Questions were also asked about geography and the scriptures.

Standards were very low but the inability of some children to make progress may not have lain with the child. Not all families owned anything to read and writing materials were rarer. One of the most difficult aspects of writing is learning how to hold and control a pencil. The need for regular practice was overlooked by witnesses and sub-Commissioners. A small amount of group tuition once a week was insufficient. It is likely that the girls who did master reading and writing had received some skilled teaching.

Trying to teach girls what became known as the 3Rs was not seen as important by some witnesses who thought that it was more necessary for them to learn sewing, cooking and domestic economy. Whether mining girls could learn this in the short sessions they could attend is debatable. Sewing requires good hand-eye co-ordination and correct holding of a needle before any progress in the task can be made. As with writing, substantial practice can be needed to master these basics. Girls who could sew and knit are more likely to have learned at home under the eye of a mother or grandmother. It is unlikely that girls could become proficient cooks without practising with ingredients and cooking equipment that were not provided in schools.

Mining girls were little different from girls from other working families in the amount of formal education which they received. Though the number of women and girls who could read and write was low there is no reason to believe that they were less able, motivated or achieving but they faced exceptional problems from their hours of work and its intensity and few maintained anything beyond very rudimentary skills. The girls who did develop them were offered few opportunities by society to utilise them.

✳　　✳　　✳

The physical condition of mining children was considered sufficiently important for data about height and build to be collected. An in-depth study of health was not required. Scriven was the only sub-Commissioner professionally competent to understand health. He did not identify any functional or organic diseases in children that was caused by their employment though the females he saw were young girls. Franks commissioned reports from doctors about the health of miners from the cradle to the grave. Symons was interested in health issues and obtained statements from several doctors and involved some in his visits to collieries. Evidence from these various perspectives gives a glimpse of the health of female miners at various stages of their lives.

The reports from Scottish doctors revealed the effect on adult women of years of work in the mines. Distortion of the spine and hips was common, brought on by repeatedly carrying heavy loads on their backs. Some older women may have suffered from osteoarthritis brought on by repeated stress on joints. Osteoarthritis of the knee is now recognised as an industrial disease affecting coal miners. Jane Peacock Watson described bearing as crushing the haunches, bending the ankles and making women old at forty.

For younger women, distortion of the spine and pelvis could create problems when giving birth. Doctor Symington thought that mining women experienced more problems in this respect than women from other working groups.

Miners in England had noted the same issues. John Bagley said that he could tell women who had worked down the mine as they were rarely as straight as those who had not. David Swallow observed that girls who moved coal at the surface and were not athletic and robust stooped forward and had internal complaints. He thought that many of them died in childbirth.

Women miners did not suffer from the same illnesses as men, as these were caused by different types of work. It was rare for women to report symptoms such as bad breath or black spittle. They were not hewing coal and not close to the loose shards that damaged lungs. Several women reported weak muscles or pain in various parts of the body, which they attributed to overwork. It is possible that they were suffering from osteomalacia which is a form of rickets.

In physical appearance, mining girls looked very healthy as they were generally well-built and muscular. This was caused by the work, which developed strong muscles. The Craven sisters and Ann Ambler were slender girls who did not develop strong fibres. This attracted no comment from Scriven who identified by measuring that only four per cent of children were of this delicate build. He was also silent about the developing plight of seventeen-year-old Sarah Jowett who complained that her back now hurt because she was too big for the passages, considering her healthy but sullen.

Symons took his instruction to obtain information about the physical condition of children seriously and had fifty collier girls measured for height and girth. He did the same for fifty farm girls from the same area. Comparing the girls in each year group his samples prove the contention that miners had shorter height and were bigger in girth than other workers. The farm girls were generally taller than collier girls, especially in the mid-teens though in the later teens the gap was less. At the age of sixteen female miners could reach a height of 5 feet and 1 inch or more. This was not short for the mid-nineteenth century. Measurements of girth showed that although young mining girls were stockier this was much less apparent after puberty.

Of particular interest in Symon's investigation is some data for Dewsbury, where the heights of the girls at given ages are noticeably less than the average computed for girls in other pits. Some of these girls had been working for several years, which points to a relationship between the length of time worked and growth retardation. At the time, the cause of this was thought to be the effect of working in cramped passages.

The actual cause, deprivation of natural light, was identified to Symons by Dr Sadler. Vitamin D is needed to produce and maintain strong and healthy bones and growth. It forms in the body after exposure to sunlight. A deficiency of this vitamin can cause rickets, a disease characterised by soft bones and skeletal deformity.

A different point demonstrated by Symon's data is that collier girls tended to be taller than boys until their mid-teens. This suggests that puberty was not the only determinant of the point at which some witnesses thought girls should stop working underground. It was also the point at which a boy of the same age would probably have caught a girl up in terms of height, strength and maturity and would become a more valuable asset as he grew strong enough to assist with getting.

Symons was a shrewd observer of health. He noted that there were some painful exceptions to the healthy appearance of most collier girls. These included the Margerson sisters, all of whom were delicate. Mary Day looked pale enough to elicit a question about her health.

William Irving the incumbent of Bolsterstone church considered that mining children were healthy. His view was contradicted by Symons who reported that those he had seen in the area appeared to be suffering ailments and colds. Symons attributed the unhealthy appearance to hurrying with the belt and chain but it is more likely that the cause was linked to poor ventilation. Irving typified many professional witnesses in not making any effort to understand the reality of a local industry for those who worked in it.

Like Franks, Symons tried to establish from doctors the effect of mining on health. He uncovered a range of opinions, demonstrating that medical science had not developed sufficiently to provide any definitive conclusions. Yorkshire doctors had little experience of the effects of protracted working in mining on women, as the occupation was increasingly confined to girls. They tended to the opinion that girls were unlikely to suffer long-term effects from working underground if they worked in good pits and left after a few years. The degree of independence of the doctors was a factor in their opinions. Those who had strong connections to employers were more likely to consider underground work healthy or, at least, not harmful.

✳   ✳   ✳

An accident can change someone's health permanently in a moment. Pit accidents happened frequently. The Scottish doctors revealed that minor accidents were a very regular occurrence and one which was far more pervasive than is apparent from the women's testimonies. Many were scarred as the result of deep cuts and grazes. Dust led to eye problems as well as breathing difficulties. Within witness statements are references to accidents, which would have had long-term effects for the hurrier but appear to be regarded by the women themselves as minor inconveniences. The hallmark of a serious accident was something that prevented or interfered with work rather than something that might have caused permanent disability or disfigurement. Personal distress arising from this was not referred to. A woman kept her feelings to herself.

Accidents fell into categories. Most were the result of inadequate attention to safety on the part of owners and workers. They would now be seen as preventable with proper equipment, training and supervision and the enforcement of safe systems of working.

Ann Stevenson, Rosa Lucas and Mary McQueen had limbs crushed or broken by falling roofs or rocks. Ellspee Thomson was no longer able to work after a stone crushed her leg and foot. Phyllis Flockhart had the flesh torn from her leg whilst moving rocks and was off work for seven weeks. She was able to have medical treatment as the colliery owner always paid for doctors to attend workers injured underground.

In Scotland, bearers fell off ladders or the straps of the crail broke, shedding the load onto the person following them. Margaret McNeill injured both her legs when she fell off a ladder.

Women were injured by corves, often because the corves ran out of control. Even empty trucks could be heavy and could gain speed on the return journey to the face. John Oldham's wife was knocked down by a full tub of coals and then run over by the wheel. She was ill for three months. Betty Harris climbed on top of a wagon to get out of the way of another one. When the one she had clamboured onto set off unexpectedly she was crushed between the coals and the roof and off sick for twenty-three weeks with damaged hips.

Others were less lucky and suffered permanent damage from accidents. Martha Wood was knocked down and run over by a corve, which led to spinal curvature and hip disease. Despite the pain, she worked for almost three years after the accident until the agony became too much and the mine owner gave her a recommendation for the infirmary where she stayed for four months. Catherine Thompson's knee was crushed by a hutchie and became malformed. She was in great pain after working all day.

Hands and feet were maimed regularly. Jane Johnson's hand was crushed by a stone and she lost a finger. Margaret Hipps had lost a finger on her left hand and Janet Dawson lost the tips of two fingers. Fourteen-year-old Mary Brown, who worked with her two brothers to support their widowed mother and younger siblings, had to hobble back to work with an injured ankle that gave her trouble, as the boys could not manage without her. Janet Brown and her two sisters developed sore feet. Two of them found it too painful to wear shoes. Ann Fern had her leg broken. Edward Bennett's mother almost lost an eye when she was cut by a pick. Isabel Wilson's cheekbone was smashed by flying coal. John Marsden reported a girl who got burned in an explosion of firedamp. Patience Wroe bore the scars of fire on her face for life after setting her hair on fire with a candle flame whilst pushing a corve.

Accidents were only one cause of health problems. Minor cuts and scrapes happened daily and could be the source of untold misery if they became infected. Within two months of starting work nine-year-old Margaret Archibald had a badly infected foot that was discharging pus and her spirits had been broken.

Pits that were wet had distinctive hazards. Ann Fern's feet were made raw by water. Alice Kershaw's legs swelled so badly that she had to leave and on the 1841 census she is reported as at home sick rather than working. Alice Gaskell had boils on her back and legs eaten with water. Rosa Lucas thought that water had once eaten the flesh from her legs. Margaret Winstanley had to work in 18 inches of water at times. She felt this had caused a recent illness that had kept her in bed for several days and made her baby poorly.

Leptospirosis is an infection caught through contact with water which has been contaminated with rat urine and that can enter the body through a break in the skin. Mild forms of the infection can resolve themselves without medical attention. It is possible that some girls in wet pits could have contracted this illness.

Fanny Drake worked in a wet pit at Flockton and reported that she often had headaches, colds, coughs and sore throats. Flu-like symptoms are produced by leptospirosis and it is possible that Fanny was suffering from something more sinister than a cold. At a time when apparently minor ailments were not an acceptable reason for staying away from work, if the family needed the wage a sick girl would have to continue to work unless she was physically unable to do so.

Headaches can result from exposure to gases that are present in underground rocks. Five of the eight girls working at Cardwell and Haigh's badly ventilated pit at Dewsbury had headaches which were caused by the blackdamp within the pit. Mary Gledhill became unconscious on one occasion and it caused Mary Ann Wild to have a cough.

Sally Margerson suffered from headaches and nosebleeds. She sometimes bled from her mouth though this only happened at work. The cause may have been blood vessels that ruptured under the strain of pushing corves with her head.

Specific problems occurred at individual pits. Jane Snaddon nearly died and was off work for seven months after drinking the water underground when she became too hot. She had contracted a severe bowel complaint, possibly dysentery. Girls at the pit where Margaret Gormley worked were prone to bellyache suggesting that they might be in contact with contaminated water.

Missing from the report is any sense of psychological illness though it is likely that some girls were affected by the accidents that they witnessed and sometimes were involved in. Rosa Lucas had to walk past the place where her father had been killed and sometimes fancied that she saw something.

For some the mine proved a healthier place of work than their previous employment. Helen Weir and her sister tried and left factory work because the dust from the fibres made them hoarse and the long hours standing caused their ankles to swell. The hours were less in the pits making the work that much more acceptable. Scriven reported families unconnected with the mines who sent children who suffered from bronchial and pulmonary illnesses to work underground in the warm and humid atmosphere rather than outside in the biting air. This was reported to restore some to health, though no named examples of this are cited.

One of the biggest issues for women working underground was pregnancy. No concessions were made to the woman. If the family could not do without their work, some women had no choice but to struggle underground almost until the last hours before confinement. This was widespread in Scotland. In Lancashire, Betty Wardle reported giving birth underground and carrying the baby up in her skirts.

Kennedy commented on the number of babies who died, considering it great, even in context of the infant mortality rate at the time. He may have been accurate in his observations. A mother debilitated by heavy work and an insufficient diet may not have produced good quality milk for her baby. Women working underground would have been exposed to a variety of noxious gases, similar to those ingested through smoking cigarettes. Twentieth-century research identified lower birthweight, respiratory problems and susceptibility to cot death as enhanced risks for the babies of mothers who smoke.

Another risk facing pregnant hurriers was miscarriage. Doubtless many babies were lost in the early weeks of gestation without anyone other than the mother knowing about this. In Scotland there are numerous references to false births, in which not only was the baby lost but the mother's health was significantly compromised also. Miscarriages were extremely serious as they left the mother too weak to return to work for several weeks, if at all. The cause of this was likely to be that not all the products of the failed pregnancy had been expelled from the womb, leaving problems of bleeding or infection. Women bearing live children were often back underground within ten days.

The longer term effects of underground work on women's health are unknown. Some former miners lived to old age with no obvious effects from their work. Rebecca Whitehead died aged eighty-three in 1874 of old age after one month's illness. It is not known how long she had been a miner. Ann Eggley died aged sixty-two, which was a good age for the time. She had worked in the pits for eleven years. Her sister Elizabeth lived to be seventy-one. Her death certificate recorded bronchitis for two years amongst the causes of death suggesting that working underground may have had a long-term effect. Harriet Craven lived to be eighty-four and Dinah Bradbury to seventy.

Other girls died not long after leaving pit work. It is thought that Esther Craven and Hannah Bowen died in 1844. The causes of death are not known.

When pits were dry and well-ventilated the sub-Commissioners concluded that girls who left the mines after a few years generally escaped ravages to their health. The five women listed above tend to validate that hypothesis. What the sub-Commissioners did not take account of were the repeated minor injuries that women and girls regularly sustained. The reality was that women's health and well-being was harmed by their work underground almost daily. If they were lucky, the injuries were bruises that would fade and cuts that would heal, even if they left a scar, possibly blue with coal dust. Beneath the healthy physical appearance of many of the girls interviewed by Scriven, Symons and Kennedy a darker picture was hidden. Franks witnessed it first hand when he saw how the extreme labour of bearing coals could break the body of an adult woman over time and the spirits of a child almost immediately.

CHAPTER 9

What Not To Wear
Clothes, demeanour and morality

I have a coarse shift and a pair of trousers on always in the pit as I
have now.

Margaret Westwood, 14, hurrier

The manner in which mining women and girls supposedly dressed
shocked the influential classes in May 1842. The Commissioners painted a
scandalous picture of females who wore trousers and worked topless.
Their report omitted to provide any context to the evidence it cited or
how common these practices were. Instead, it propagated an urban myth
that half-dressed young girls working underground were gradually corrupted by their surroundings until they became depraved and degenerate
creatures, devoid of womanly feeling and incapable of bringing up
children in good ways. It was powerful imagery but the reality was less
sensational.

The belief that mining women worked half-naked underground and
men wore no clothes was not new when the sub-Commissioners investigated. In 1813, a pamphlet produced by Richard Ayton after a visit to a
Cumberland mine had sensationally described them working in this
manner. At that time no one in authority had seen fit to ensure the allegation was investigated further. Almost thirty years later, Ayton's assertions
were probably known to some of the sub-Commissioners and the witnesses they interviewed.

Clothing in Victorian times was formal in style for both sexes. As gentle-
men of standing, the sub-Commissioners and their clerks would have
toured in the socially accepted attire of the age; trousers, shirt, waistcoat
and jacket, probably topped by a frock coat that reached the knees, a
cravat around the neck, a top hat and gloves. Scriven discovered that such
formality was immediately off-putting to witnesses and to overcome the
suspicions of the workers he wanted to talk to he kitted himself out with a
flannel suit, clogs and knee protectors and went underground to observe
what happened in a mine.

Well-bred women dressed in a similarly decorous manner. Dresses
were nipped in at the waist and had full skirts that encircled a large

circumference by the time they reached the ground. Bodices buttoned to the throat, lacy collars surrounded the neck. Outdoors, the ensemble was topped by a shawl or cape. A lady wore gloves, a bonnet tied under the chin with ribbons, and may have carried a parasol to protect her complexion from the sun. In polite circles the only flesh that was socially acceptable to reveal was that on the face and, if indoors, the hands also.

Children were dressed in a formal manner from an early age, though the styles were simpler and a girl's dress might be topped by a pinafore. For younger girls, hemlines finished above the ankle.

Outfits had many layers. Beneath their outer dress women wore petticoats, chemises, shifts, bodices, stays and corsets. They served the dual function of supporting the weight of the dress and of providing warmth. Middle-class ladies wore clothes made from good quality cotton such as poplin or good quality wool such as merino. The predominant shades were red, orange, yellow or brown; colours that could be produced easily from natural dyes.

The clothes worn by working women and girls were simpler in design and plainer in colour but followed similar principles of decorum, covering the entire person. They were made from the same types of cloth as those worn by the more prosperous. This happened earlier in the century when the price of cotton goods fell making them more affordable to workers. It brought a major advance in personal hygiene as cotton was easier to launder than wool enabling workers to wash their clothes regularly. This was especially necessary for mining families whose working clothes quickly became engrained with dust, sweat and muddy water if the pit was a wet one.

The materials worn by workers were of inferior quality to those purchased by richer people and may have chaffed their skin. The shoddy and mungo industries that developed in Yorkshire in the 1820s recycled waste yarns or small fibres into cheap cloth. This was a boon to workers and made clothes and household furnishings more affordable, especially for women who could sew.

Away from work, mining lasses followed the fashions of the time if they could afford to do so. John Millington had seen them with their bright buckles and gay ribbons as jaunty and well-dressed as any other women in the town. In Scotland, some girls knitted or sewed their own clothes. Others embroidered or made lace and sold it, spending the money they received on clothes or ribbons.

At work the situation was different. Women dressed for the job and prioritised convenience and safety. Many Lancashire and Yorkshire hurriers wore trousers or breeches that stopped around their knees. On their tops they wore shirts, shifts or jackets, stout clothes to protect them from knocks and scrapes underground. Some wore neck scarves. Mary Glover spoke of always wearing a pair of sturdy breeches. She probably had to replace them regularly, as rubbing against rocks and chains would wear them out.

The public reaction to reports of women and girls wearing trousers was one of horror. The practice was widely decried as unnatural, unwomanly and indecent. Witnesses were more circumspect in their views, recognising why women dressed as they did, and few referred to it unless asked. Proprietor William Bedford thought it looked bad to see a woman working in trousers. Reverend William Irving found it painful to see girls in trousers but appreciated that it was the most convenient form of dress for the work they were doing.

He was correct. Women hurrying with the belt and chain could not have managed if they had worn skirts. For Betty Harris, hauling a corve uphill with nothing to grab hold in places would have been dangerous and possibly indecent in a skirt. Flapping material could become trapped by the corve and torn off, revealing the woman's lower body.

No matter how disgusting the sight of a woman hurrying on all fours in trousers appeared to observers, the sight of a woman using the belt and chain over a skirt would have been far more horrifying with skirts being pushed high up between legs. Trousers preserved modesty by minimising the amount of flesh revealed, even if they did hint at the outline of the female's figure.

In parts of Yorkshire, the conditions seem to have dictated what women wore and several reported working in conventional female attire. Those pushing trucks could manage in skirts. The Margerson sisters wore petti-coats, shifts and stays. The wet rag hanging around Susan Pitchforth's waist was the remains of a shift. Elizabeth Jackson, Betty Sutcliffe, Sally Fletcher and Selina Ambler wore breeches. They worked in an area where pits could be damp. In wet conditions trailing skirts would soak up water immediately. A girl wearing breeches that stopped at her knees might succeed in remaining relatively dry for part of the day.

Whilst it is possible that females were not insensitive to conventions about clothing, even underground, it is more likely that cost was a factor in what they wore. The shirt, sturdy breeches and stout clinkered shoes worn by Ann Eggley may have cost more than £1 a year. Wearing up old clothes was cheaper than buying special ones.

In Scotland and Wales, contemporary illustrations show women wearing skirts, although some were shorter than would have been considered respectable away from the pit. In these areas hauling a corve with a belt and chain was not common. Where it did happen the chain went over the shoulder rather than between the legs. Females who worked at the pit-head wore skirts.

The working clothes worn by adult women were made from strong and comparatively durable materials. They were probably uncomfortable to wear. Scots girls wore dresses made from coarse hemp which absorbed water and had to be left at the pit-head at night to dry. The dresses were hardly ever washed.

Young girls may have had to work in hand-me-down clothes. They reported wearing a variety of attire ranging from old shifts and chemises to bed gowns. That Scriven discovered so many badly-clad youngsters working underground was probably thrift. In view of the number of wage earners in the Barrett family it is unlikely that the rags worn by Mary and Ruth signified poverty. Symons commented that the working clothes of girls were generally extremely good, though he too noted some youngsters wearing old night clothes.

Scriven made much of the bedraggled state of Susan Pitchforth, a ten-year-old thruster who was interviewed by him straight from the mine, wearing only a wet and filthy rag that hung around her waist. It had once been a shift. It is possible that it had been wrecked at work that day as her statement mentioned a fall. The under-steward interrupted the interview and tried to take Susan away as her appearance was not decent. Scriven marvelled at the double standards that considered it acceptable for a young girl to work topless in rags underground but not to be seen in them above ground.

It is possible to interpret this differently. Susan spoke to Scriven before she had put on her outside clothes. Workers were properly covered on their way to and from the mine but before starting work they removed their outer clothing and left it at the pit-head. The shock caused by a half-naked girl chatting to the sub-Commissioner may indicate that partially clad females were not a norm.

Miners' daughters who worked underground often wore gold jewellery, either neck chains or little earrings. These were said to be the way of distinguishing girls from boys. It may have been a rite of passage present given to a girl when she first went underground. It indicates that some mining families were not abjectly poor or they could not have afforded the ornament. Lancashire women wore red or blue glass beads.

Whether or not they wore jewellery, girls had some kind of covering on their head. Close-fitting hats were especially useful for keeping coal dust out of their hair. Peggy Lowe who was praised for her neat and tidy appearance wore two, a low-crowned hat and a close-fitting cap. Edward Newman described the typical attire of mining girls as including a kind of skull cap. Thrusters needed a padded cap as they often needed to push with their head as well as their arms. Patience Kershaw pointed out the bald patch on her head caused by thrusting. Others developed soft and painful patches on their scalps despite the padding.

A pair of stout shoes was essential for keeping feet safe, especially in pits that had rails. In wet pits workers hurried bare-footed but this was dangerous. Dropped coals and stubbed toes could cause painful, if short-term, injury. On a daily basis walking on rough and uneven floors hurt. Particles of dust, dirt and stone lodged between the toes leading to inflammation and infection. The skin under the feet became hard. In extreme cases feet became too sore to tolerate shoes.

❊   ❊   ❊

One of the biggest differences between working families who were considered respectable and those who were not was their appearance when not at work. This linked to the condition of their clothes and whether they had the motivation to wash. Barnsley solicitor Edward Newman and Hindley's relieving officer, Mr Birchall, each spied on girls with naked legs or almost nothing on but a shift and an under petticoat washing themselves at the doors of houses. That girls had to wash in semi-public places was not indecency on their part but a function of house size. Whilst the statements of Mr Newman and Mr Birchall reveal the false respectability of some middle-class witnesses, they also prove that girls who worked underground made an effort to look clean and respectable even in difficult conditions.

Occasionally, girls were seen with tide marks round their necks and it was suggested that some women only had an all-over wash at the weekends. Again this indicates that working in a semi-clothed state could not have been a norm. Sturdy working clothes would protect the skin from too much coal dust and make it possible not to have a full wash every day. It is hard to believe that women could have tolerated several days' coal dust on their upper bodies.

Franks was shocked by twenty-year-old Christy Mitchell and her older sister who had not washed or changed their pit clothes even though they had been out of the mine for some hours. He also noted that their cottage was in a filthy condition. Their little sister Janet gave the game away by informing him that Mother drank when Father was out and he drank when he got back. Franks never considered whether their working clothes were the only ones these girls owned. Some Scottish mining families were so poor that the only clothes they had were those they worked in.

Sub-Commissioners commented about the well-dressed, comely and respectable appearance of collier girls and the number who spoke about washing themselves after work demonstrates that mining families aspired to high standards. For those who were not as well-washed or dressed as they could be exhaustion or poverty was a significant factor.

If there was one negative characteristic about the appearance and behaviour of pit girls it was that some of them were prone to using bad language at work and sometimes in banter on their way home. Co-workers in Lancashire referred to the manner in which women swore whilst at work and sub-Commissioners reported that they had heard coarse and vulgar language from teenage girls underground.

It is unsurprising that this happened. Children are apt to mimic adults and given the brutal nature of a getter's work, some undoubtedly resorted to expletives when they hurt themselves or met with problems. In Cumberland, an unnamed boy told the Commission that he had heard of God because the men damned him very often. Infinitely sadder was the evidence of Margaret Gormley that the men damned her possibly because she could not work as fast as they wanted.

Hurriers also suffered injuries that hurt and in busy pits they had to be assertive and make sure that they got their proper turn to hook their corve up to be drawn to the surface. It may have been easier for girls working alongside boys to conform to any pit norms about language.

The recorded words of the women and girls interviewed do not contain coarse or vulgar language. Even though this may have been omitted from the published evidence, sub-Commissioners regularly made comments about the witness at the end of their statement. There are no indications that they found that any female's vocabulary inappropriate. It is unlikely that bad language was universal amongst pit girls and those who may have indulged in it understood that it was not to be used outside the working environment.

The Commissioners linked the clothes women wore at work and the language they used to female morality, using the flimsiest of evidence gathered in the field. To drive the point home the report and its appendices contained illustrations showing a few partially-clad females and naked males along with detailed technical sketches of mines, shafts, winding gear and pit clothing. It was the first time pictures had been used in any Royal Commission report and it proved the adage that a picture says a thousand words.

Even today these images retain a power both to fascinate and to revolt. Women and girls were portrayed bare-breasted. It was a short step to asserting that such immodesty was the inevitable result of girls working with men who wore no clothes at all and that this led to sexual immorality underground.

Many references to female workers being almost naked were quoted out of context. Witnesses usually added except for their petticoat or chemise.

Whilst it may have shocked observers to see females wearing half the number of layers expected by polite society, mining women were not revealing any more flesh than was dictated by their working conditions.

Hurrying was a dangerous occupation that led to cuts, bruises and scrapes. It is more likely that women wore clothes that covered as much skin as possible rather than that they chose to expose it deliberately or unnecessarily. Other than a couple of isolated examples the evidence for women working partially clad is hearsay. The fact that moving a heavy corve caused a hurrier to get very hot is a salient point when considering them.

Lancashire miner John Millington claimed to have seen many a woman working with her breasts hanging out. This demonstrates that the women were wearing something on their tops although he does not indicate what the garment was. When they became too hot they probably unfastened a couple of buttons at their neck or loosened their scarf to try to cool down. In doing this a woman bending forward or moving on all fours would expose cleavage. Half-dressed female workers was not a point that Kennedy made. As he made some underground visits to mines where adult women worked, it is likely that if women were working without proper tops he would have witnessed the practise and commented on it.

Symons was the only sub-Commissioner who observed females working topless and it was a solitary example. It occurred at the Hopwood pit in Barnsley. By coincidence, he selected this pit as an example of a medium-sized colliery and included details of its workforce in one of his tables. From this data and the statements he took it is possible to work out who were the topless female miners who scandalised the country.

The pit employed six females, Maria Mallender a young trapper, and five hurriers, Ann and Betty Mallender, Elizabeth and Mary Day and Bessy Bailey. During his visit, Symons went underground and saw four of them naked to the waist. Elizabeth Day was wearing her top as she was cold. Evidence from women at other pits corroborated that hurriers were often hot whilst pushing but cold when standing still. Symons found the group at the bull stake, which was an area where the full corves were pushed to before they were hauled to the surface.

When he realised that the group of topless adolescents he was talking to included girls, Symons asked how the sexes could be distinguished and discovered that the only way was by their developing breasts. He was shocked by the hilarity the answer generated. The notion of gender difference was probably irrelevant to anyone in the mine and the hilarity may have hidden their embarrassment at his question.

From the statements of the girls it appears that Elizabeth and Mary sometimes worked in their tops. Three girls usually worked without them,

Ann and Bessy who were fifteen and eleven-year-old Betty, an undersized girl 3 feet 10 inches tall.

Some of the girls had family members employed at Hopwood. Elizabeth and Mary's father and brother worked there as did Bessy's brother. The prevailing atmosphere may have resembled the safety of the extended family and was not a nursery of juvenile vice as presumed by Symons. All the girls at the pit reported going to Sunday school or chapel as did the boys who were interviewed. It was not lack of moral guidance that caused any of them to dress immodestly.

Symons noted the unusually onerous nature of Elizabeth Day's work as she had to manoeuvre full corves uphill for part of the way without any help. Other girls may have had to push uphill on their routes. This would have been extremely hot and sweaty work. Being too hot can lead to heat exhaustion and heat stroke, serious health conditions. In his report Symons commended Elizabeth Day for her good feeling and propriety. Taking her top off at times to cool down does not seem to have made her unfit for respectable society.

The Hopwood episode branded a few teenage girls and the boys they worked with as corrupted creatures. Poignantly, and unknown to the Commissioners, before the report was published, the Mallender sisters and Mary Day died in an underground explosion.

Symons' visit to Hopwood took place two months after his visit to Hunshelf where he first encountered girls working underground and had been revolted by belt and chain hurrying. He was sensitive to situations that he thought demeaned women and seems to have set himself a mission to do something about it. In the next weeks, he pointedly questioned witnesses about the clothes women wore at work. He did not discover any other pit where females worked with bare tops, which suggests that the situation at Hopwood was exceptional.

Elsewhere in Yorkshire, Scriven portrayed female hurriers as more than half-naked. The example that he provided, somewhat indirectly, was Ann Ambler who worked at Ditchforth and Clay's pit at Staniland. He produced a sketch representing her being raised out of the mine by a winding woman at the end of the day, a procedure he claimed to have observed. She was sitting across the lap of a boy named William Dyson. Both were wearing only breeches. Victorian society was shocked by the drawing of two topless teenagers of opposite sex sitting crotch to crotch, with the boy's arms around the girl. Ann's clothing, as drawn, was at variance with the written evidence in the report. When Scriven saw Ann, he noted that she did not wear shoes or socks and her thighs were bare. He made no comment about her not wearing a top, which is surprising as, had that been the case, she would have been almost naked. At fifteen she was five years older than Susan Pitchforth about whose topless state he remarked a few days later.

The thigh extends from the hip down to the knee so Scriven probably saw a girl who wore breeches that finished above her knees, not one who was uncovered almost to her hips, an interpretation that was subsequently put on this illustration.

The sketch was probably not drawn at the time of his visit and was intended to illustrate the dangers involved in winding workers to the surface using a primitive winch rather than to be an accurate representation of Ann Ambler in her working clothes. Its realism can be questioned in other respects. It is debatable whether the woman operating the winding gear would have been strong enough to haul two teenagers in the manner shown and the rope may well have broken under the strain. Whether Scriven was conscious of its propaganda value when he drew it is an intriguing unknown.

A more usual situation which Scriven and Symons each observed was naked men hewing. Men worked without clothes in some pits to try to stay cool, a practice which Scriven had witnessed in Staffordshire where women did not work underground. In the Yorkshire pits, the reason for nakedness may have been water, as some getters wore singlets or waistcoats. It is probably the reason why men worked without breeches in the Bolton area. Men working without clothes rarely happened in Lancashire in pits where females were employed. Women threw stones at a naked getter and refused to go anywhere near him. It suggests that, rather than lacking morality, mine workers of both sexes regarded men working unclothed alongside adult women as an unacceptable practice.

In Yorkshire, the impropriety of young girls working where they saw naked men was widely felt. Some of the girls interviewed were clearly unhappy about this and some miners and owners recognised it was not a pleasant situation for teenage girls to be placed in. John Sharp, the steward at Bowling, a pit that did not allow females, said it would be wrong to have girls as they would have to mix with naked men.

Scriven and Symons treated men working naked as proof that immoral conduct between the sexes must take place at work. Symons found about a dozen witnesses who confirmed this, but the majority of their evidence is either hearsay or opinion and he only unearthed two credible examples of sexual immorality underground. Matthew Lindley spoke of sexual intercourse regularly taking place at the bank between a married getter and the girl who hurried for him. Joseph Ellison referred to a getter who had repeatedly attempted to rape his stepdaughter, until she was no longer able to come to the mine. These examples have an air of authenticity and represent contact that would have had more risks attached to it above ground.

Most females were working for a father or brother who would expect the coal to be moved and would quickly sort out anyone trying to take his daughter or sister away from her work. A getter who was employing a female as his hurrier could dismiss her and employ someone else if she did not keep her attention on her work. Mining was hard, cramped and difficult. Most getters and hurriers were primarily interested in completing the day's quota and getting outside again.

Lancashire miner John Bagley appears a reliable witness. He confirmed that men took indecent liberties with women underground but not regularly. John Oldham reported that it was usual for single men to have connection with the lasses that drew for them but he was referring to courting or cohabiting couples rather than sexual activity that took place below ground. Mr Hilton, a pit steward from Wigan, spoke of a violent disturbance the day before Kennedy's visit, which arose from a collier neglecting his wife and taking up with the girl who drew for him in the pit.

Pit owner Mr Roscoe provided Kennedy with alleged examples of immoral conduct, which he suppressed as unfit for publication, suggesting that he did not give them much credence. Kennedy posed the question of whether men took indecent liberties with women to several witnesses, including to married women. That he did not emphasise sexual immorality in his report suggests that he did not consider it a major issue.

Bastardy amongst mining girls was also perceived as an issue by middle-class witnesses but no sound evidence was produced. The relieving officers of Wigan and Upholland, Mr Halliwell and Mr Harrison, believed that girls had a great number of illegitimate children but that they were rarely presented for parish relief. They attributed this to mining women knowing that their wages were too high for them to be eligible. An equally credible reason would be that mining women were not having vast numbers of illegitimate children. Benjamin Mellor, a pit steward at Silkstone, felt that there was less immorality in the pits than in service. Colliery manager John Sutcliffe declared that there was no bastardy in his pit. Illegitimacy amongst Scottish miners was reported to be low because of the value children had as future workers.

Some witnesses believed that mining girls were no more likely to have illegitimate children than girls in other forms of work or born into other working families. They did not try to make any link between the perceived lack of moral education and the sexual behaviour of girls. Several pointed out that although pregnancy before marriage often occurred, the father would marry the girl and no one would think the worse of her. Birth and christening records for working-class families in the nineteenth century show that many marriages took place when the bride was pregnant or even after she had borne the couple's first child.

Evidence for higher rates of illegitimacy is difficult to trace in the 1841 census. Lone mother Mary Lockwood in Silkstone had a two-year-old son but she was a widow. Ann Eggley was a few weeks from her wedding when she gave her evidence. Birth records and census returns for future years give no indication that she was pregnant or had an illegitimate child.

Sexual morality was too delicate a subject for the sub-Commissioners to discuss with women so it is one where their attitudes and perceptions are not recorded. A few children indicated that they were illegitimate with fathers having deserted the mother. Phyllis Flockhart had also been deserted by her mother and was taken in by her aunt. Mary Brown had a married sister who had been abandoned by her husband after the birth of their first child.

Symons and Scriven were intelligent men, capable of forming evidence-based judgements, yet their comments about sexual morality underground overstated any evidence they had discovered. As a barrister, Symons should have been conscious that evidence given by several witnesses was hearsay.

It is not difficult to understand why both men thought the practice was more prevalent than it actually was. They had seen men working naked and each had seen a female without a top. Immediately after Symons' visit to Hopwood, John Thorneley JP, a mine manager for forty years, confirmed this was a regular practice. With apparently reliable witnesses corroborating their observations, the issue was not something they could conclude to be occasional.

That Symons and Scriven highlighted their evidence in the manner that they did may have been the result of consultation with two of the Commissioners, Doctor Southwood Smith and Mr Saunders who visited three Yorkshire pits with them in June 1841. They made a visit to the Hopwood colliery where Symons discovered girls working naked to the waist and to Waterhouses at Elland where Scriven had found Susan Pitchforth dressed in rags. The other pit was Swan Bank where conditions resembled a city drain. It is unlikely to be coincidence that the pits where the Commissioners were taken were some of the worst discovered. Had Symons discovered the girls in ripped trousers at Meal Hill before the Commissioners came it seems probable that Southwood Smith and Saunders would have been taken there also.

The visit to Yorkshire may have been arranged at the request of Symons and Scriven and it is likely that they discussed their findings with the two Commissioners and were told to spare no details and to emphasise the morality issues. This would explain why Symons' and Scriven's reports play more to the emotions than those of the other sub-Commissioners and focus on matters which are not reported on by them. Southwood Smith had experience of how reports from Royal Commissions were viewed by the establishment. All four men would have known that calls for reform of workers' conditions based on compassion were likely to be countered by arguments that Parliament should not become involved in regulating economic matters.

All the investigators who witnessed women and girls working at mines were shocked by labour that was too severe for a woman's strength and the dreadful conditions they worked in. If they wanted to improve the woman's lot they needed an argument that trumped economics. In Victorian times that argument was morality.

CHAPTER 10

Publish and Be Damned
The impact of the Commissioners' report

At what age do you intend to turn us out of the pits? Put me down
for fifteen years old. I should like to be turned out.

Dinah Bradbury, 19, waggoner

When all the evidence was collected each sub-Commissioner had to produce a formal report for his district. It seems likely that their clerks left
them with a written transcription of the witness statements at the end of
their local visits. The clerks may have spent their evenings writing out the
notes that they had taken during the day and collating any other papers
that witnesses provided. Hinted at within the district reports, and probably accounting for some minor discrepancies between the reports and the
witness statements, are personal notes made by sub-Commissioners which
have not survived.

Some reports included the date and address of the writers, indicating the
different social milieu they inhabited. William Wood lived at Singleton
Lodge, a handsome house near Bury. The census recorded Jelinger Symons
at Victoria Square in London and John Kennedy at Ardwick near
Manchester. Scriven and his wife were staying at a hotel in Halifax,
though they normally lived near London's Regent's Park.

The four Commissioners took the lead in collating the district reports
into a formal document that covered the whole country. Ashley's primary
interest lay with the children who worked in unregulated industries such
as earthenware and porcelain, needle and pin-making, bleaching and
paper-making. He spent part of 1841 leading a committee that reviewed
the Factory Act and attempting to include children who worked in the silk
industry within its provisions. His knowledge of mining was slight and he
first descended a mine shaft in September 1842. As he noted contacts with
Southwood Smith, Horner and Saunders in his diary he probably received
verbal briefings about the nature of the evidence that was being unearthed.

Three of the Commissioners made the effort to understand what mining
entailed. Horner spent a day with Kennedy. Saunders and Southwood
Smith visited some thin-seamed mines in Yorkshire, and two thick-seamed
ones in Leicestershire.

The district reports began to trickle back to the Commissioners from April 1841. A number of them contained technical illustrations to clarify points that were hard to convey in words. Some were produced by sub-Commissioners and others were obtained from mine managers.

The first to be received was Scriven's report for North Staffordshire, a relatively uncontroversial document that gave few hints of the shocks to come, despite his discovery of men working naked underground and the offensive odour from their excessive perspiration. Wood's followed at the end of the month, generally favourable to mine owners, though with a fair-minded approach to miners. One witness suggested that somewhere in the vicinity a few girls worked alongside naked men but Wood did not pursue it as a topic for investigation or draw any attention to it.

Kennedy's report was undated but as he completed his investigation at the end of May, the report is unlikely to have been any earlier than mid-June. It contained eleven drawings that are cross-referenced in his text. They show workers hewing, moving tubs of coal and trapping. Three of the sketches were produced by Horner on his visit. The others are believed to have been drawn by a Manchester geologist, Edward Binney, at Kennedy's invitation. One of them illustrated the evidence of Betty Harris dragging a corve uphill.

Kennedy concluded that the work of females in mines was of peculiar severity and unsuited to their physical condition, especially those who were mothers. He considered that the nature of the work below ground tended to demoralise and brutalise the females employed, prevented attention to domestic duties and diminished their competency for the proper care and training of their children. He identified no countervailing advantages to mining families or to the public to compensate for the disadvantages.

Kennedy's condemnation of women working underground is signifi-cant. He had no sympathy for miners who he portrayed as a caste apart, devoid of any civilising virtues and a potential danger to public order. He considered that the choices they made rather than the nature of their work caused all their undesirable characteristics, pointing out that they were above ground more than they were below it and that they routinely over-stated their hardship. That he was sufficiently appalled to step outside his remit and state that there was no justification for women working under-ground is a very strong indictment of how dreadful that work was.

Symons' report for Yorkshire was completed at the beginning of July 1841 and Scriven's probably around the same time. There were many similarities in their approach and content, which suggests that the pair agreed a strategy for presenting information about females. Both are highly emotive on this point, an unusual approach for intelligent, professional men and a great contrast with their measured observations about shocking safety practices. Both men produced a report for a different district in a more dispassionate style. Scriven included a number of sketches, whilst Symons had technical drawings.

Scriven described the debased condition of females before stating that he would be a traitor to his countrymen if he did not attempt to inspire the Commissioners with a desire to rescue females from a state of moral degradation and suffering to which they were doomed. He then quoted several girls who had told him they hated mining and would prefer other work.

The report included ten drawings that Scriven is believed to have produced. Two of them illustrated mine-workings. The other eight were controversial and were widely copied in the weeks that followed the publication of the national report. They comprised the sketch of Ann Ambler, three of the backs of naked coal getters illustrating the positions in which they worked, a topless hurrier using the belt and chain, two clothed hurriers moving trucks and an adult female wearing trousers and a blouse scooped low at the neck. One of her breasts is partially exposed.

There was no reference within Scriven's investigations in Yorkshire for topless workers hurrying with the belt and chain. He met naked male harnessed hurriers in Staffordshire in pits where females did not work. The woman with an exposed breast appears to illustrate the evidence of John Millington, which Kennedy took in Lancashire.

Scriven's reason for including images for which he had no textual evidence is unknown. That he saw the events he illustrated but did not record them in his report is one possibility. The other is that the pictures were imaginative representations.

Symons linked the employment of females underground to a negation of Christian values and one that shamed a civilised country. He reported in line with the brief he had been given but devoted three pages of his report to examples that amplified his concerns, presenting his evidence as discussions of moral condition, prostitution in pits and oppressive female labour. His techniques of leading his readers to his desired conclusion were subtle where the corroborating evidence was weak. He never stated that immoral conduct was occurring but his prose requires a very careful reading to identify that he was conjecturing that it must happen, not stating any fact that it did.

The shock tactics adopted by Scriven and Symons consciously played to the sensibilities of the age and described situations that were incapable of defence. Whilst they may have overstated their evidence, it is worth remembering that bad practices relating to safety within mines expressed in balanced, measured and factual tones failed to engage interest.

The analysis of the evidence for the national report began in earnest in Autumn 1841. In October, as Franks began a hasty investigation in South Wales and reports from some of the tardier sub-Commissioners began to arrive, the secretary of the Commission was tasked to make some brief visits to confirm that there were no issues with female labour in a few areas that had not been well covered.

Two reports were submitted by Franks in December 1841. The descriptions of coal bearing were the most searing examples of oppressive female labour that were discovered and added to the breadth of the evidence. He also included pictures. For Scotland he illustrated the statements of Janet Cumming, Margaret Hipps and Katherine Logan. A picture of an aged woman bent horizontal at the waist under a heavy crail of coal conveyed more graphically than any words the horrible and obscene nature of that drudgery. Two other sketches show a young bearer carrying coals along a passage and two bearers on a ladder as the top one's load slips onto the girl below as described by Agnes Moffatt. For Wales Franks produced a sketch of a barely-clad male hurrier using the belt and chain. Females were not employed underground in the county where the man worked.

Franks concluded that the employment of females in mines was degrading in that other classes of operatives would not marry girls who worked in the pits, painful because it was totally disproportioned to the female strength and sex, unnecessary because the evidence showed that strong lads did the work much better, and immoral because it was inconsistent with the proper discharge of the maternal duties and with the decent proprieties of domestic life. He identified the exclusion of females from mining as a solution to some of the wider social problems he had noted.

The Commissioners faced a dilemma as they had been charged to provide information, not to make recommendations for change. As the ugly evidence piled up they decided to produce two reports, one into mining and another covering the other industries. They identified mining as an industry that was virtually unknown, carried out in places wholly removed from the public view and inaccessible to those who did not work underground and decided to concentrate on this for the first report. This indicates the depth of their disgust about practices within that industry, as Ashley was anxious for information that would support his on-going campaigns for factory reform.

The decision to produce two reports enabled them to accelerate the publication of the evidence relating to mining. Although a laborious task, the Commissioners analysed all the information they received, grouping it according to topics and classes of witness and then presenting it, district by district, under the headings they had asked the sub-Commissioners to report against. The speed with which the report was produced was remarkable given the amount of data they had received. It shows the seriousness with which the four men approached their work.

✳   ✳   ✳

Their report was long, deliberately sacrificing conciseness in favour of listing multiple examples of similar horrors. It was supplemented by the publication of two appendices, in which were included all the district reports and the transcription of all the witness statements.

Other than visiting a few mines the Commissioners did not formally verify the evidence that had been presented to them. They took the view that the similarity of evidence from witnesses in similar categories in different areas was confirmation of accuracy.

Much of the text of the national report can be traced directly to the district reports and several extracts from Franks, Kennedy, Scriven and Symons were reproduced verbatim, along with corroborating comments taken from the evidence of individual witnesses. It is difficult to believe that no one identified that some of the statements were supposition or hearsay, especially as Wood had alerted them to the fact that the middle-classes had little knowledge of the lives of miners.

The report included illustrations from the district reports, presenting the degrading labour more forcibly than any verbal descriptions. The impetus for this innovation came from Southwood Smith, who thought that parliamentarians who did not have the time to read the entire report would find time to look at the pictures and grasp its main messages. The illustrations were produced by woodcut, a method of printing in which a drawing is outlined on a piece of wood. When the wood is chiselled away on either side of the lines an edge remains standing proud of the block. Ink applied to the block coats the edge but not the areas chiselled away. When paper is pressed against the inked wood the picture is transferred. Within days of their publication a handful of sketches of minimal artistic merit became some of the most influential woodcuts ever made.

As the work of adult women was not part of the inquiry, the Commissioners circumvented the difficulty by including the evidence about it as aspects of moral condition or oppressive labour. They linked the inability of adult women to look after a home or family to the fact that children were reported to be growing up without civilising moral guidance in a comfortless home. Much of this was already in the public domain, as the inquiries into textile factories had identified that women who worked in factories became deskilled and deficient in performing domestic duties and sometimes coarse in speech.

The sensational new information was that miners worked in a state of perfect nakedness and were assisted by females of all ages, these females being themselves quite naked down to the waist. Several witnesses from Yorkshire and Lancashire were quoted to support this point, an interesting one being seven-year-old William Cooper who said that the women in the mine were nigh naked as they wore trousers and had no other clothes except loose shifts.

The emphasis on indecency reflected the information the Commissioners had received and that they believed that it was an accurate portrait of the industry. Scriven and Symons genuinely thought that in some areas the sexes mingled underground wearing negligible clothing and that the practice existed much more widely than they had managed to identify. Some owners had refused to co-operate with the sub-Commissioners and it was easy to assume that they had dark practices to hide.

The perceived opportunities for promiscuous sexual misconduct to occur underground rendered the situation unacceptable to a middle-class whose thoughts quickly jumped to illegitimacy and possible claims on the poor rate. The Victorian conscience was tardy in considering whether it was morally acceptable that young girls obliged to get a living should have to encounter naked men whilst they did so.

Preoccupation with nakedness at work had existed before the report was published and at least one correspondent had drawn it to Ashley's attention. A letter in *The Times* in October 1840 from one of his supporters, using the nom-de-plume the Children's Friend, referred to workers in the calico printing industry labouring half-naked and the children sometimes running outside in this state. The report tapped into an existing public concern when it focused the spotlight on this point.

The Commissioners realised at an early stage that the inquiry had discovered practices, that ought to be eradicated. When four investigators of very different personality and viewpoint spontaneously exceeded their remit and advocated intervention on behalf of adult women it was impossible for them not to try to ensure that change occurred. The manner in which the national report was presented shows that none of the four Commissioners wished to exceed his own instructions by making recommendations. What was open to them was to present all the information they could find in a way that would horrify the consciences of the middle-class, a group whose opinions were becoming increasingly influential.

Tooke, Southwood Smith, Horner and Saunders approved the report on 21 April 1842 and it went to the printers. Knowledge of its controversial content was rife in political circles and the Home Secretary, Sir James Graham, considered how to prevent it coming into the public domain. In frustration Ashley arranged for copies to be leaked to newspapers that were favourable to reform. They included *The Morning Chronicle* and *The Times*. Then a misunderstanding took place in the Home Office which resulted in a copy of the report being placed on the table of both Houses of Parliament.

Copies of the report were made available to interested parties. Rapid dissemination of the contents was assisted by illustrations, which simultaneously aroused the wrath of the middle-classes for the flouting of public decency in the mines and the anger of aristocratic mine owners who regarded them as nasty depictions of practises that they did not recognise. The first picture, taken from Scriven's report, was of the hurrier harnessed by a belt and chain. The picture was immediately seen as a bare-breasted female but it may have been misinterpreted. The hurrier's face looks masculine and the supposed female breasts may have been a clumsy attempt to illustrate well-developed pectoral muscles on a male. Miners developed muscular strength in their upper body.

If the gender of the hurrier was misconstrued no one was likely to correct the mistake in view of the immediate groundswell of public opinion that females should be banned from mining. When details and then pictures of topless females appeared in the press the ensuing outpouring of public disgust gained Ashley a propaganda advantage that he could only have dreamed of.

The first mention in Parliament was in the House of Lords on 5 May when the Bishop of Norwich drew attention to the report. Concerned that if the Bishop's speech became known about the public might think that girls worked in the collieries in chains, Earl Fitzwilliam laboriously explained for the record that the chain was merely used to draw the vehicle containing the coals.

The scandal broke to the wider public on 6 May when *The Morning Chronicle* ran a feature about the report. It was closely followed by *The Times* with a feature on 7 May drawing attention to the manner in which children were worked. Another followed on 14 May highlighting the vicious treatment meted out to children and Harriet Craven was mentioned by name. On 17 May the paper turned to consideration of women underground, quoting from the evidence of Betty Harris dragging her corve uphill and highlighting that men worked naked in west Yorkshire and females wore little other than a pair of broken trousers.

The *Guardian*, at that time a Manchester paper, first covered the report on 14 May. It focussed on females, nudity and pauper apprentices and called for legislative remedies. The article generated little public discussion. On 21 May a letter from Z, a mine overseer, disclosed that although the

126

correspondent disliked females working in mines he was equally opposed to the legislature involving itself in regulating labour.

Initial newspaper coverage was a factual representation of an inquiry that pulled no punches in exposing bad practices. As regional newspapers and periodicals picked up the story the coverage became more sensational. Some evidence was quoted out of context, purporting to prove the frequency with which the sexes worked side-by-side whilst scarcely clad. Pictures were commissioned which re-interpreted the original drawings. Sketches of naked miners bordered on erotic and the picture of the female in trousers with an exposed breast was translated into an image of unambiguous sexual invitation. The picture of Ann Ambler and William Dyson was reworked into images that emphasised the sexual connotations of the posture. No one wondered how the young workmates felt about being forced into such close bodily proximity whilst they were being hauled out of the mine.

The written word began to diverge from the text of the report and workers became naked rather than partially covered. People who had not seen the original text believed what they read in their papers and periodicals and moral outrage grew. Editors discovered how to push the boundaries of truth and use salacious content whilst claiming their motivation was to protect from the vices it illustrated.

Whilst descriptions of the moral and physical horrors endured by women and children and the plight of the pauper apprentices circulated the country along with calls for reform, many in Parliament sat on the horns of a dilemma. Remedying the situation meant that owners would have to invest capital to improve some mines to induce men to work in them. Employing men would mean paying higher wages. If ponies were used for underground haulage they would have to be bought and fed. The outcome would be more expensive coal.

For industrialists, this would increase the costs of the goods their factories manufactured. Landowners who had leased mining concessions would lose their royalties from mineral rights if mines shut because they were unaffordable to work. Public morality and private economics clashed and it was not clear that those who had the power to remedy the situation had the will to do so.

Almost as soon as the report became public Ashley stated his intention to introduce legislation to eradicate the abuses but it was almost a month before this happened. Politicians who felt unable to state any opposition to reform manipulated parliamentary procedures to prevent him from having the opportunity to speak. He finally managed to move a bill on 7 June 1842 in a speech to the House of Commons, which lasted over two hours. This was very late in the parliamentary session and Ashley took a risk by introducing it. Bills which have not passed all their stages in both the Commons and the Lords automatically lapse at the end of a session and have to complete all their stages again in another session. Two months before the session ended was a very tight timescale and some may have thought that the wasted month had delivered sufficient delay.

Ashley was a talented and persuasive orator and when he was able to surprise his colleagues with new evidence he could carry a debate by eloquence, as he had done on the night he had requested the Royal Commission. His speech was well-constructed, balanced and focused on drawing evidence out of the report. His references to nakedness were not great which suggests that he realised that some of the evidence was supposition. He used as his examples Susan Pitchforth and Mary Holmes, girls whose partially exposed flesh sub-Commissioners had witnessed. He referred to the horrors of belt and chain hurrying, pregnant women underground, long hours, the oppressive labour of coal bearers and the lump of coal flung at Harriet Craven.

Ashley's bill contained four points. He wanted to ban all females from working in mines and all boys under thirteen. He wanted to prevent the apprenticeship of paupers and prevent anyone under twenty-one from winding people into or out of the mine. The early stages of the bill passed unopposed on the strength of Ashley's speech but three of its clauses were controversial and as the initial wave of revulsion produced by the report faded mine owners began to question the impact of the proposed measures. Although there was little serious opposition to the provisions relating to females, restricting the work of boys and apprentices would remove a substantial amount of cheap labour from the mines. This would have translated into a higher cost for coal.

On 15 June, the *Guardian* commented that the proposals would be severely felt in districts where a large proportion of females were employed and where there were no other means of employment. It recognised potential damage to the coal industry in Lancashire and stressed the need for both parties to be able to state their arguments fairly.

By late June opponents were questioning the accuracy of the report and the railroad speed at which the bill was progressing. In the House of Commons, Peter Ainsworth challenged the evidence of an unnamed little girl whose story was disputed by the owner of the mine who had made enquiries amongst his workmen about her. She was reported to have died.

It is unclear which girl was being referred to as Ainsworth was in contact with owners in Lancashire and Yorkshire, though any owner learning of Margaret Gormley's beatings at the hands of workmen might be presumed to have looked into the matter. The point at issue was not whether the girl's evidence was truthful but that it had not been taken in front of a magistrate on oath and was inadmissible.

Ashley steered his bill through the House of Commons on 5 July 1842 but it had to complete a similar procedure in the House of Lords where it was not well-received. Ashley had difficulties in finding a peer who was prepared to sponsor it. Most were reluctant to oppose the Marquis of Londonderry, who began to unleash the full force of his fury against the bill even before it left the Commons. The Duke of Buccleuch, who had excluded females from his mines, agreed to lead it but then had to decline because he held government office. Finally the the Earl of Devon agreed to become its sponsor.

The Marquis of Londonderry, who had substantial interests in coal mining in the Durham area, saw the report as inaccurate and Ashley's proposals as a threat to the industry. He set out to prevent the bill becoming law. In a series of vitriolic attacks over several days he attempted to have the issue referred to a select committee for further consideration and impugned the integrity of the sub-Commissioners for the underhand manner in which they had collected evidence. He even opposed the banning of females from underground work, arguing that some seams needed women as it would be impossible to use horses. Other lines of attack included predictions of beggary and starvation and whether poor law boards would think it right to support at parish expense women who could work underground. He challenged the Earl of Devon to name those mines where immoral conduct took place. The Earl rose to the occasion by asking for details of seams that could not be worked without women. Neither man could have given a satisfactory answer.

It is sad that Londonderry was unable to rise above the personal and see the report as an attempt to improve industry standards, rather than an indiscriminate attack on all mine owners. The Marquis claimed, possibly without too much hypocrisy, not to recognise the industry that was portrayed. He argued that the sub-Commissioners had disproportionately concentrated on bad practices within a small section of the industry and had failed to give due acknowledgement to good practices. In reality some large mine owners were commended for standards which were good at that time and for the interest that they took in improving the workers' lives. Had the sub-Commissioners applied what is now known as as the Pareto Principle and concentrated on visiting the few mines which employed the largest numbers, the abuses and horrific practices discovered in the smaller and the badly managed pits would not have come to light.

Despite Londonderry's uncompromising approach other peers were more measured in their opposition, recognising that as the press was ranged in favour of change it was better for the bill to fail through parliamentary process rather than direct opposition. Lord Radnor pointed out that women working in mines was dying out of its own accord and asked why a ban was necessary. Lord Devon read the mood of his opponents and took a pragmatic approach, conceding several key points that he knew would not be passed in order to secure others.

In the course of its discussions, the House of Lords made some interesting observations about women in mining but these were not examined in any depth. Some of them were perceived as obstructive comments that deserved no serious debate, such as whether immorality occurred in other industries and whether legislation was needed to prevent the overcrowding of workers' cottages. Two peers tabled amendments to enable adult women who were already working in the mines to decide for themselves whether they wished to continue in this work. These were rejected as any hardship resulting from exclusion was considered to be temporary.

It would have been helpful if the position of adult women had been discussed sensibly and in detail as the bill was considered. The economic difficulties that women could face when there was no alternative local employment were highlighted by the Duke of Hamilton whose mines were in such an area. Unfortunately, owners who predicted starvation for displaced women were opponents of reform. They were seen to be motivated by self-interest rather than concern for workers and the points they made were quickly silenced.

It was disingenuous of supporters of the bill to argue that all females would immediately find a new source of income or that their families could afford to keep them. Parliament let some vulnerable women down when it decided that the principle that females should not work underground was more important than acknowledging any individual hardship that this might cause.

When slavery was abolished those economically affected received compensation. Whilst it is unlikely that public financial support would have been granted to impoverished women, the 1840s were a time of private philanthropy and charity. Raised awareness that some women would experience problems that were not of their own making may have inspired benevolently minded members of the middle-classes to become involved in assisting them to find other work, or relieving the distress of those who were not able to do so.

The mutilated bill was passed by the House of Lords on 6 August 1842. The changes had to be ratified by the House of Commons. Ashley faced a personal dilemma as he considered that his intention to protect boys had been invalidated but days before the end of the parliamentary session, ranged against a hostile House of Lords, and with a government not interested in helping to secure his original proposals he reluctantly decided there was nothing else he could do to achieve them.

The rewritten bill was accepted by the House of Commons and on 12 August 1842 it received Royal Assent, becoming known as the Mines and Collieries Act.

Ashley's achievement was much more significant than his own gloomy assessment suggests. He forced a bill through Parliament in extraordinarily quick time despite the private views of important parliamentarians that his proposals should not become law. He established the principle that Parliament would intervene in the working arrangements of adults. By setting the age at which boys could begin working underground and limiting the length of pauper apprenticeships, he reinforced that workers who lacked equal bargaining power would be protected from unfair treatment.

Lord Devon's contribution has often been overlooked but his ability to apply pragmatism to temper Ashley's more idealistic aspirations ensured that meaningful legislation was passed. Had the bill been lost in July 1842, Ashley might never have succeeded. The summer recess would have bought time for opponents to get to grips with the mass of contradictions that inevitably existed within 2,000 pages of evidence and force a further enquiry to ascertain the true facts before any reform could be contemplated.

Throughout the three months of scandal, debate and compromise there were few who seriously opposed preventing females from working underground. Middle-class opinion regarded a woman who was forced to work outside the home for money as an object of pity. It was thought that the men in some families were responsible for this outrage because they would work for only a few days each week themselves and condemned wives and children to work to increase the family's income. Measures that enabled a woman to fulfil her ordained roles of tending to her home and family and instilling proper moral values in her children were thought to be what a respectable woman of any class would want. It was considered that men working more regularly would replace the woman's lost earnings.

Amongst workers there was also support for the measure. Against a background of economic hardship labouring men saw women working outside the home as a threat to their jobs and incomes. The Chartists and the Ten Hours committees that agitated for factory reform sometimes demanded that women's work should be restricted and certain occupations reserved for males. Friendly and provident societies established in this period often prohibited women from becoming members.

The only people who were opposed to the exclusion of women from underground work were a few mine owners who knew that improving conditions in their mines was expensive, and women and their families in areas where they knew that there was no alternative employment available. Ashley considered that he sacrificed the children to save the women. He would have been surprised to realise that a number of women had no desire to be saved.

CHAPTER 11

What Katy Did Next
The impact of the Mines Act

You must just tell the Queen Victoria that we are guid loyal
subjects; women-people here don't mind work but they object to
horse-work and that she would have the blessings of all the Scotch
coal-women if she would get them out of the pits and send them to
other labour.

Isabel Hogg, 53, former coal bearer

According to the information received by the Commissioners, around 6,000
females were affected by the new law. The figure can be ascertained by
totalling the number of female miners listed in the sub-Commissioners'
district reports and making allowance for the incompleteness of the returns
they received from employers.

The figure of 2,350 is often stated as the number of women who were
engaged in mining in 1841. This figure was extracted from the census
returns and reported to Parliament. It was quoted by the socialist writer,
Frederick Engels, in his book, *The Condition of the Working Classes in England
in 1844*. It achieved a wide circulation because of the popularity and influence of Engels' book and for many years the more accurate number disclosed by the Commission's report remained hidden from view.

During the debates in Parliament in 1842, the number of females working
in mining had been mentioned and it is interesting that the discrepancy
was not queried a couple of years later when the analysed census information was available. Other than for a brief period in the spring and early
summer of 1842, female miners held little interest to Victorian society
and the impression that had been formed of them was negative. Anyone
privately identifying the difference between the two figures may have been
grateful that the problem was much less than it had appeared.

The understatement within the census had many causes. Workers
viewed the census enumerators with discomfort. This was the first time
officials had attempted to collect the names, ages, occupations and place of
birth for the entire population and many were worried about the use which
would be made of the information they gave.

Arousing further suspicion was the fact that the enumerators were local
men such as teachers, clergymen, parish clerks and relieving officers who

might be involved in deciding applications for outdoor relief for a sick miner or an older member of his household. Claims for help would be unsuccessful if it was suspected that other family members were receiving a wage.

Irrespective of their occupation, many heads of household played safe and did not mention that wives and children were working. Some enumerators misunderstood their instructions about recording occupation and only listed what the head of the family was doing. As a result, the employment of women and children outside the home in any occupation was understated across the country.

Mary Glover, Catherine Landels, Mary Ann Lund and Martha McNeill were amongst the few female witnesses whose occupation was recorded in the census. Patience Kershaw was listed as a labourer but with no indication of the type of work she did. For most female miners, as far as the official records were concerned, their labour went unacknowledged.

✳   ✳   ✳

Excluding females from the underground workforce was planned as a three-stage process. From the date the bill became law, no female who was not already working underground was to begin employment. All girls under eighteen had to cease working within three months. The date of 1 March 1843 was set as the date from which no woman should go underground to work. This was seen as a necessary measure to allow owners an opportunity to improve their mines so that they could be worked by men and ponies. It also gave women an opportunity to adjust to the changing situation.

The date by which adult women had to stop working underground was a subject of debate before and after the act was passed and some peers advocated a longer period for transition. In July 1842 Lord Campbell attempted to silence any further discussion with the statement that for a woman even a workhouse would be preferable to the slavery of a mine.

Petitions from women in Lancashire and Scotland who did not agree with this standpoint were received by Parliament until early in 1843 with assertions that starvation and even prostitution could be the fate of women displaced from mining in places where no other work was available. In February 1843, Stirlingshire MP Mr Cumming Bruce gave notice of a motion to amend the Mines Act to allow adult single women and widows to choose whether they wanted to work underground. He was denigrated in *The Times* for condoning women having to drudge underground to keep their men in meat and gin instead of the intention of nature being fulfilled by men working to support their families and women being free to bring up their offspring. Ashley described the proposal as a charter for living in sin. Bruce received little support and his amendment was lost. The idea that some women did not have a man to support them was not understood.

Excluding women from underground work was a rushed piece of legislation, carried on a wave of emotion, whose wider implications were not thought out by those who advocated it. The belief that change could be effected without causing hardship for anyone who was deemed to be the deserving poor came from an uncritical reading of the evidence collected by Franks, Kennedy, Scriven and Symons. None of the four was qualified to offer a professional opinion on the matter and they had not collected sufficient evidence to permit anyone else to form a balanced view.

Kennedy attempted to identify the practical consequences of excluding women in a discussion with Lord Balcarras' agent. He was told that it would be difficult to make any quick change to female labour north of Wigan because of the number of women who would be affected. This did not support his own opinion, so he hedged his argument by saying that whilst violent change should always be avoided it was necessary to make a stand against such a pernicious system.

It is difficult to criticise the Commissioners and sub-Commissioners who saw women and girls struggling underground for drawing attention to labour that was beyond their strength and attempting to devise a remedy. Ashley's motivation in fighting for an immediate ban on any female work underground may have been tinged with other considerations. Although the principal advocate of factory reform for almost ten years, he had not secured any improvements in workers' conditions and he needed a high-profile success to demonstrate his own credibility amongst his colleagues and his opponents. Preventing the moral corruption of women and girls was an easy argument to win.

Ashley carried out his role as president of the Commission at arm's-length. He received the final draft of the report early in April 1842, a month before it was published, and was very conversant with its detail by the time he introduced his bill. He was well-placed to identify that sub-Commissioners had received warnings about introducing change too quickly in some places, that some women were the sole source of support for their families, that some were unmarried and that most who spoke of hating mining also spoke of needing to earn some income. If any warning bells rang, he silenced them.

The majority of pits complied with the law and excluded females by the required date. In some cases they were ones that were already progressing towards a male workforce and the Mines Act accelerated the transition. The owners of these pits were often very active in helping the females who were affected to find other work. Some provided a small weekly allowance until a job became available. At Flockton local mine owners gave employment as servants to some girls.

Amongst aid given to females were classes to help them learn household management and sewing. A notable example of this was the Walkden Moor Servants' School which was set up in 1843 by the Egerton family to train local girls in the skills needed to become domestic servants. It was noticed that the pit girls who had most difficulty in obtaining other work were the ones who lacked practical skills. Besides helping girls who had worked underground the school also offered places to orphaned daughters of colliers. The school took twelve girls as boarders. As well as learning to read and write they were trained in the duties of housemaid, laundry maid and scullery maid. By 1846, sixteen girls had been placed in service and the school received regular applications from local people looking for servants.

In a few pits females continued to work as hurriers and bearers as though no legislation had been passed. This took place across the coalfields. Underlying similarities were that the females were usually adults who did not have a male member of the family to support them and the locality was economically under-developed with no alternative work available. Some of the women were responsible for supporting dependants. They arrived at pit-heads, day after day, begging managers to let them work, sometimes being turned away, sometimes managing to slip underground without being noticed. Where mines had more than one entrance it was difficult for the manager to police them all. Deterring some females from trying to work often meant blocking up secondary entrances.

A few unscrupulous owners and managers were not concerned about the law being flouted. It is likely that most who turned a blind eye to women working acted not out of defiance but because they realised the acute distress suffered by these women and regarded allowing them to work underground as a way of assisting.

In some areas, women continued to work without problems until the end of 1843. The Mines Act was flawed as there was no effective method of enforcing its provisions and no will at government level to ensure that it was complied with. The Home Secretary had the power to appoint an inspector to check whether the law was being observed but this did not happen until November 1843.

Appointment to the vacant post was made to resolve an entirely different controversy, one caused by civil servant Hugh Seymour Tremenheere's critical report of educational standards in Wales in 1839. The Government needed to quell the furore his report continued to provoke and arranged for him to be promoted to the vacant role of Inspector of Mines. It was a questionable motivation and one that demonstrated indifference at the highest level as to whether the Mines Act was complied with. Tremenheere, a barrister by training, had no experience of the mining industry. He had no secretariat to support him and a remit that comprised around 2,000 working pits. Some were in remote locations and were difficult to visit. He had no power to issue instructions or to prosecute offenders.

Despite the inauspicious circumstances, Tremenheere was effective in his role, securing almost universal compliance with the law within four years. He also laid the foundations for a more rigorous attitude towards workers' safety in mines. He took his new responsibilities seriously and adopted a pragmatic approach to the difficulties that faced him. He was conciliatory but persistent and tried to secure compliance by influence and persuasion before resorting to harsher methods. The mere fact of his appointment indicated to recalcitrant owners that the law could not continue to be ignored and Tremenheere dated some of their belated efforts to prevent women working underground to his announcements of impending visits.

Tremenheere spent several years visiting mining areas, usually ones where there were considered to be problems, assessing how the law was being complied with.

Beginning in summer 1844, he presented an annual report to Parliament, commenting on the main aspects of his work and on the conditions in mining communities. The annual reports reflected some of the difficulties experienced by women forced out of work. Despite the high-profile coverage in 1842, the country quickly lost interest in the lives of female miners and the problems they faced were not widely reported in the press. The influential classes had no answer to the reality that a measure designed to secure the public good created individual hardship of exceptional severity for some women.

Tremenheere's reports demonstrate that age, family structure, place of residence and former occupation all had an impact on women and their families. What the reports do not provide is any sense of how much distress occurred in many households where husbands, sons, fathers and brothers were considered able to support their unemployed female relatives irrespective of their own level of income. Nor is it possible to identify for how long any distress persisted.

Those who were considered to be benefiting from the change were married women with young families. The view of the middle-class was that any privation caused by reduced income was more than offset by a comfortable home and the care of the children, which the woman could now attend to. One unnamed mother at Pencaitland considered that as more than half her earnings had been spent on childcare, laundry and repairs the loss of spending power was not great. The implications of the loss of income for the woman who looked after the children and the washerwoman were not addressed by Tremenheere.

The extent to which individual families suffered depended on the number of females whose work was no longer available. Those who had an adult male in work and boys who were able to assist him were reasonably placed to earn sufficient to maintain the family, especially in pits that the owners had improved. Collieries identified different effects from the change. The Bannockburn colliery added three pence per ton to the men's wages to try to compensate them for the loss of female labour. The Devon colliery thought men had benefited as the cost of hiring a strong male to move trucks was less than the cost of two girls. Families with a large number of boys were very supportive of the new law and anxious for it to be observed, identifying the opportunity to improve their own income as their sons took on the work given up by females.

In the short-term, most mining families experienced reduced standards of living. Tremenheere met a number of women who were resentful of their enforced idleness and that their ability to feed and clothe themselves decently had been taken from them. Healthy, unmarried girls in their late teens and early twenties appear to have been particularly angry about the change.

In a number of cases the hardship was temporary. If other industries existed locally, even on a small scale, it was possible for females to obtain employment, though the pay would not have been as much as they earned as hurriers. In west Yorkshire a number of girls were absorbed by the woollen mills. Parts of the Firth of Forth had work available. Tranent had a paper industry. Around Edinburgh there were openings for female servants. Dunfermline offered woollen mills and there was brick-making at Dalgetty. Where pits were set in rural locations seasonal work could be found in agriculture. Some Welsh mines were co-located with foundries. Near Wigan, some young women dressed in male clothing and went to work as labourers for a road builder.

Even if vacancies did not exist in numbers, some men working in factories would have been attracted to hurrying by the higher income it offered them and the possibility of learning to be a getter. This in turn would have increased the openings available for women.

Mr Gibstone, the manager of the Newbattle colliery, employed sixty females and assisted half of them to obtain jobs in the local paper mills. He told Tremenheere that the colliery had been planning to dispense with female labour. His evidence to Franks a few years earlier indicates that in 1841 there was no such intention. The determined efforts made by this colliery to ensure that no female was left in want by the enforced change demonstrates the intention of many owners to comply with the new law, even if they were personally opposed to it.

Girls under eighteen had to leave underground work in November 1842. This may have caused severe distress for Harriet Morton and Fanny Drake whose wages were supporting the low incomes of agricultural labourers in areas of little alternative work. The Craven sisters, supporting an impoverished weaver, may have been able to find immediate work in a mill although Harriet's hours would have been restricted. Getters who employed girls who were not relatives would have seen only risk for themselves in not replacing them with boys as soon as they could. Those who employed relations may have been prepared to take the risk.

The group that experienced the worst problems were unmarried adult women. It had been assumed that all women had a man who could maintain them. The reality was that the majority of female miners were unmarried. A few of these were widows supporting their children or young adults keeping their aged parents. Some were young girls contributing to the family income for a widowed mother.

When women's jobs disappeared, entire families saw their income reduced to subsistence level or below. Widows, orphans and old, infirm or disabled members of households may have been eligible for parish support in their own right but the amount was very low. The system was at its harshest in Scotland as no allowance was available to any person considered fit enough to maintain themselves as it was presumed that they could obtain work.

Most owners were not indifferent to the women who were displaced from their pits and took steps to help those who were exceptionally needy. This was usually interpreted as those who had no one else able to support them or who were supporting others. Roles above ground were found for some. The Wellwood colliery in Dunfermline rotated pit-head work amongst the most destitute families with eight sharing the available work in 1844. The Carron Company found work for twenty women who had no other source of support, dismissing some men in order to employ the women.

Despite the best endeavours of some motivated employers it was impossible to assist all needy women. Some of them displayed a surprising degree of initiative and turned to self-employment, even though it only brought in a fraction of their former wages. Those who were able to sew or knit made items to sell, sometimes hawking their wares door-to-door. Two unmarried sisters in their forties began manufacturing and selling camstone, a clay-based product used for cleaning stone floors. At the time, self-employment in an endeavour that demanded physically hard or unpleasant work was seen as a pitiable way of making a few coppers and a sign that a woman lacked the qualities needed to secure and hold down a job. From a modern perspective, the entrepreneurial efforts of these ageing sisters in the face of adversity indicates a spirit that had not been eroded by years of work underground.

＊　＊　＊

Although opponents to the Mines Act had predicted several problems, one that came as a surprise affected a number of elderly workers in Scotland. It was not replicated in other parts of the country where the age of female workers was younger. Women who had laboured in a pit for perhaps fifty years had few skills beyond the knack of moving heavy loads of coal and minimal ability to learn to do anything else. Those who were capable of working were probably suffering from impaired health and minor disfigurements caused by their work. Such women were unlikely to find other jobs, especially if they were competing against younger women in areas where there were few vacancies.

Tremenheere was moved by the plight of elderly women who had been deprived of their former means of livelihood on moral grounds in order to benefit future generations and who were not likely to find an alternative way to maintain themselves. He hinted that public assistance should be made available to them. It was a hint that elicited no response. The only known exception was an anonymous benefactress who sent £100 to Ashley to be spent to relieve distress, to which Ashley added a contribution of his own. Women received between 5 and 10 shillings so that they could purchase clothes or shoes.

The living standards of displaced older workers fell to a very low level but most appear to have avoided penury. Those who were considered too ill to do any work obtained a pittance from the parish. Those who were unable to secure other work were assisted by family, neighbours and private philanthropy from their former employer. Scottish miners often worked for one colliery all their lives and it was not unusual for owners to assist workers who had served them for many years. The Fordel colliery took some widows onto its own poor list and provided them with food until their daughters found employment that was sufficiently well paid to support the girl and her mother. Recognising the scarcity of work in the area, the colliery also supported a few girls with food until they found jobs.

In 1851 the census recorded that Margaret Douglas, a widow of sixty-seven, was a pauper coal bearer living with her unmarried daughter, Janet, who became a travelling messenger after leaving mining. Isabella Wilson, aged sixty-three, received parish relief to supplement the coppers received from her lodger. Seventy-one year old Elizabeth Campbell, a retired coal bearer, was supported by her son. For the women who surmounted a few difficult years after 1843, their situation in 1851 may have been little different to what it would have been if they retired from mine work at a time of their own choosing.

Coal bearers found themselves in a very difficult situation if they worked in pits that owners believed could not move coal by any other method, as males were not prepared to take this type of work. Many may have found themselves pressurised by their families to continue mining either because no other assistance was available or because it was unaffordable. In 1844 Tremenheere discovered that Reverend Beresford, employer of Margaret Leveston, the youngest bearer interviewed in 1841, had made no effort to prevent females from working. He extracted the strongest of assurances from the clergyman that arrangements would be made to prevent further breaches of the law. The arrangements appear to have been successful as subsequent censuses reveal that coal mining in the area did not decline until the 1860s, when it is likely that the seams were worked out.

Tremenheere also had to obtain assurances from Sir George Clerk, a member of the government, that proper vigilance would be maintained after discovering a number of females underground when visiting his works. One of these may have been Alison Jack, the eleven-year-old whose workload had appalled Franks. In 1851, Alison and her sister made a living for themselves and their little brother by picking rags in the paper mill. Their parents were dead.

By summer 1845 Tremenheere considered that only 200 women in Scotland had not found jobs and that a similar position existed in Lancashire though the basis of these estimates is not clear. It was a comforting thought for Victorian society and appeared to prove that those who had argued that any distress caused by the Mines Act would be short-lived were right. His assertion took no account of the reduced circumstances in which families might be living and it provoked no difficult questions about how 400 women were managing to exist.

In Scotland, most of the affected females lived in poverty-stricken towns and villages along the upper reaches of the River Forth. At Falkirk, over a hundred females remained without gainful employment and up to thirty families experienced severe distress. A similar situation was discovered in Pembrokeshire in 1846 where a few females with no one to support them continued to be employed. Tremenheere recognised the economic reality of the area and pointed out to owners methods that had been used in other areas to try to alleviate similar distress.

Those responsible for a woman working underground could be brought before magistrates and a maximum fine of £10 imposed for every woman discovered. The minimum penalty was a fine of £5. Tremenheere under-stood that persuasion would not work with owners who connived at the law being ignored. In Scotland, when owners would not take proper steps to exclude females, he handed any evidence he held to the local prosecutors for them to take court proceedings. Workmen from the Redding Colliery and the Clackmannan Coal Company were each fined £5 and costs for employing females. This was a substantial punishment, representing over a month's wages. Colliery managers avoided being con-victed for connivance, arguing that responsibility for a woman being underground lay with the getter who had defied instructions issued by the mine and paid her wages as a private arrangement between them.

Some of the most widespread defiance occurred in the Wigan area where the proportion of adult women working was high and where families such as Jane Sym's had a reasonable lifestyle with her labour. With workers and owners believing that the law should be flouted it came close to falling into disrepute. Tremenheere discovered a mine-owing magistrate actively facilitating women to work in his pit.

The fate of a watchman, Mr Bradley, and a policeman, Mr Smith, prob-ably deterred any informant from laying charges or giving evidence about women working illegally. In January 1844, Bradley laid two separate charges against John Bleasdale for employing three females in his pit. He was convicted on one count and fined £5. The second charge was not heard because of an irregularity in the paperwork. Undeterred, Bradley laid the charge again, stating that he had seen Rebecca Melling come out of Bleasdale's pit accompanied by another woman and a man. Shortly after-wards, he saw a third female enter the mine. The evidence was cor-roborated by another watchman who was with Bradley. Rebecca Melling appeared as a witness for the prosecution, denying that she had been in the mine on the day in question. She was not believed and a further fine of £5 was levied on Bleasdale.

Two months later Bradley and Smith were on a night patrol in Wigan when a crowd of miners recognised Bradley. Both men were floored, sur-rounded by a large crowd and kicked from their head to their ankles. Had a few local residents not come to the rescue it seems probable that the mob would have kicked the pair to death. Both men were reported to be severely cut and bruised about the head and their bodies much disfigured. It was clear that the attack had been carried out in retaliation for Bradley giving information about females working underground. The crowd were recognised as colliers but no one named the individuals and they were not apprehended.

Tremenheere made further enquiries when informed by the magistrates' clerk that the police neglected opportunities to lay information about women working in mines. He reported his view that the police were not in dereliction of their duty, as they could not spend all their time watching mines. He authorised the employment of a suitable individual for a limited period to procure evidence on which convictions could be obtained and employed a qualified legal professional to assist in bringing cases to court. It was a pragmatic method of circumventing the intimidation of witnesses that was occurring in the area.

By funding a prosecuting lawyer and a private investigator, Tremenheere appears to have exceeded the powers given by the Mines Act. The added professionalism the appointees brought ensured that charges stuck. In October 1845, Messrs Preston and Harding were convicted on two counts of employing women. In February 1846, John Topping was convicted of employing Ellen Hughes in his colliery at Hindley and fined £5. The magistrates agreed not to proceed with charges of employing five other women on hearing that Topping would take heed of the one conviction.

Magistrates began to develop the law and it was no longer possible for owners to argue that they had given instructions or displayed a notice that had been ignored. To avoid liability they had to show that they had taken appropriate steps to ensure that their instructions were obeyed. In January 1846, Messrs Stocks and Harrison were fined £5 and costs when Martha Unsworth was employed without their knowledge and against their express instructions. The underground manager knew that she was working but had not taken any steps to prevent her doing so. Mr Evans of Haydock was fined for a similar violation. Both firms said that any future breaches would lead to the site manager being prosecuted instead of the owner.

The case that was probably the most decisive in persuading owners that the law had to be complied with was the one that followed an underground explosion at the Burgh colliery at Caphull in November 1846. Mine owner John Hargreaves, a local magistrate, had flouted the law since its inception and was reputed to be employing thirty females. Mary Booth, Jane Halliwell and Jane Moss died alongside five male colleagues and Hargreaves was prosecuted for knowingly allowing females to work underground. He evaded responsibility as miner Ralph Ainscow testified that the mine manager, Joseph Ellis, had regularly facilitated females working at the pit. He had told them to wear men's clothes and concealed them when the police were around. Ellis denied this, asserting that he had been deceived by the workers. The magistrates concluded that Hargreaves had no case to answer and that Ellis alone was culpable.

As the inquest into the deaths concluded, a juryman described how he had once referred to a young miner who regularly passed his house as a clean young fellow, only for his daughter to observe, 'nay, that's a wench'. Another juryman realised that the woman he had seen was Jane Moss.

When owners took a firm stance against women working in their mines and combined this with practical steps to ensure that they could not slip in unnoticed it became very difficult for them to go below ground. Managers needed to remain vigilant because, months or years after female labour had been dispensed with, desperate fathers would try to sneak a girl underground. Nine-year-old hurrier, Patience Wroe, was discovered when she set her hair on fire with a candle at Caphouse colliery in 1847. Following the accident, the colliery owner Sir John Lister Kay employed her as a servant until her marriage. Patience was one of eleven children and it is likely that her father was struggling to feed his family.

Like Mary Booth, who was twelve when she died, Patience was too young to have been working in 1842. Another tragic girl was thirteen-year-old Martha John who died in a fall at Moreton colliery in Pembrokshire in July 1847 as she was being lowered into the mine. Families who were desperately poor remained prepared to flout the law for many years if the opportunity arose.

The year 1848 appears to have been the point at which the number of females working underground became negligible. The most important factor may have been an economic upturn that began around that time and which gradually resolved problems caused by lack of employment. Demand for labour began to increase and the hungry forties started to recede. When women found new jobs or their family became better able to maintain them they had no need to try to cling to their former occupation.

In 1850, Tremenheere was joined by additional inspectors with practical experience of mining who asserted the right to visit underground. For several years, they occasionally discovered women underground in different parts of the country. A few memoirs and recollections published years later also suggest that some females worked underground well after it became illegal. It is impossible to know whether these stories were accurate, fabricated or merely mistaken about the date.

It is unfair to apportion all accountability for a few women working underground to mine owners. The Mines Act was the first time adults had been prevented by law from deciding their employment. A woman faced no sanction for being underground and one with a mind of her own could be difficult to detect if she was determined to work there. Dressed in male clothing she would not necessarily be picked out by a casual glance. Some mines had several entrances enabling females to slip underground and earn a wage so long as there was a man who was prepared to hire her. Underground work was better paid than any other job an uneducated woman could obtain and it is not surprising that occasionally a woman was discovered. The more interesting question is how many were not.

✳   ✳   ✳

For a few of the girls and women who featured in the sub-Commissioners reports it has been possible to catch glimpses of their lives after they left the pits. Ann Eggley married miner John Hardcastle in 1841 and lived in the Barnsley area for the rest of her life. She had at least four children. The family had taken in lodgers by 1871 and in 1881, a widowed Ann was worked as a winder in a cotton mill, apparently the sole source of support for her thirteen-year-old grandson. She died in the workhouse in 1884.

Elizabeth Eggley married miner George Goodall in October 1843 and had nine children. Elizabeth lived in and around Barnsley until her death in 1897. Both sisters now lie in unmarked graves in Barnsley cemetery.

Harriet Craven found employment in a mill and when she married Jonathan Sutcliffe in 1849 her occupation was given as a comber. Between 1850 and 1868 she had eight children, four sons and four daughters. Although the mother of a six-month-old son she was working as a wool comber in 1851. By 1861 she was a dressmaker. Any bad memories Harriet may have had of her time underground were not sufficient for her to keep her son away from mining. Ten-year-old Craven Sutcliffe, too young to work in the mills, was a drawer in the pit.

Harriet spent her life in the Bradford area. She never learned to write, the 1911 census being annotated as the mark of Harriet Sutcliffe. She had a long marriage but one which was perhaps not made in heaven. Letters between her children reveal that Harriet and Jonathan argued and were both very stubborn. She died in 1912.

It is likely that the Craven sisters never knew what had been written about them by the man who spoke to them at the mine or that their plight had been noted in *The Times* and spoken of in the House of Commons by Lord Ashley. In view of the regular assaults she sustained, Harriet may never have given a second thought to the lump of coal that had been hurled at her. Esther Craven disappeared from the records and it is thought that an entry in Bradford's death register in March 1844 is hers. Other women understood to have died young were Hannah Bowen and Ruth Fern who is believed to have died in childbirth.

Sarah Gooder's older sisters disappeared from view after the 1841 census but Sarah appears to have become a live-in nurse before marrying miner James Marsland in 1854. She had two sons and died in 1912.

In 1850, a pregnant Susan Pitchforth became Mrs Siswick. In 1861 she was living in Huddersfield. Her sister, Rose, became Mrs Marsden and had a family before she died in 1865. Their father who sat smoking whilst his shivering and half-naked daughter spoke to Scriven lived to an old age, dying in 1897. Not all miners became mashed up and died young.

Whilst positive identification has not been possible a Margaret Gormley whose details fit what is known about the Commission witness emigrated to America in 1850. United States censuses for 1860 and 1870 recorded her as an unmarried servant to two affluent families in Boston, Massachusetts.

Patience Kershaw found a job in a factory and subsequently as a housekeeper to a widower and his young family. She died unmarried in 1867.

Rachel Tinker's family gave up mining in Yorkshire and moved 20 miles across the Pennines to take up work in the cotton mills. In 1851, Rachel was working in a textile factory. It is thought that she married twice and died in 1907.

Matilda Carr and Margaret Westwood were servants in 1851 whilst Anna Hoile was a wool comber and an unmarried mother with a ten-month-old daughter. Ann Ambler still lived in the family home and worked in a mill. As Ann could read it is intriguing to wonder whether she became aware of the controversy which she created and how she felt about Scriven's sketch. Ambler was a common surname in west Yorkshire and in the following decade several girls called Ann or Hannah Ambler can be found in the local marriage records. It is possible that she was one of these brides.

Rebecca Whitehead had her work cut out for several years taking three grandchildren into her home and caring for a brother who was described on censuses as being of weak intellect.

Elizabeth Day married Edwin Rock in 1846 and died in 1849. Her widower then married a sister of her former colleague, Bessy Bailey.

Across the Pennines, Dinah Bradbury married but was widowed by a pit accident in 1845. She remarried in 1848 and brought up two sons as well as a daughter from her first marriage. She died in 1891.

Mary Glover took over the running of the family home. By 1851, her aged parents had died and four of her five children were working. A four-year-old nephew was staying with the family.

Many witnesses have vanished without trace. Garrulous Betty Harris, intelligent Harriet Morton, Mary Holmes with her ripped trousers, dignified Margaret Grant, thoughtful Rosa Lucas, versatile Alice Hatherton, and the delicate Margerson sisters are amongst those who have not been located after 1841. It is likely that some found work in adjacent areas, making it impossible to identify them on later censuses or in marriage or death records.

The later lives of women and girls whose words ring across the decades were typical of working-class women of their time. They encountered love and loss, hardship and responsibility. Some progressed from being daughters and sisters to wives and mothers and grandmothers. Others died at a tragically young age. Some brought up families, ran homes, earned incomes and became the backbone of their communities. Some may have made a life in a new county or even a new country. These were vibrant, feisty women whose lives after 1841, as much as their words in 1841, lay to rest the myth that females who worked underground were in any way degraded or defiled by the unsuitable work which society thrust upon them at a very young age.

CHAPTER 12

The New Woman
Mining women above ground

I care nothing about where I am. I should be worked hard
anywhere, I dare say.

Ann Fern, 14, hurrier

Women's involvement in mining diverged after 1842. In some places, any female employment at pits was eliminated within a generation. In other areas, women found work at pit-heads and a distinctive culture developed around them. Economic conditions and working-class thought each determined how the female role developed in any area.

Throughout Yorkshire women never gained acceptance at the pit-head. In 1841, work at the surface, like work underground, seems to have been limited. Commission witness David Swallow referred to girls working on the pit banks near Wakefield and the census captured a handful of girls working above ground at Silkstone.

The West Riding of Yorkshire was unusual in 1842 in having an alternative industry that could accommodate females excluded from hurrying. Women and girls were able to move to the woollen mills and few had to look to the pit-brow as a place to earn a living. Compliance with the exclusion was not instantaneous and in 1844 an owner from Wooldale, possibly Uriah Tinker, was fined for employing four teenage girls underground. A pocket of resistance also existed at Halifax for a few years.

Miners in the Barnsley area consolidated their early collective view against the employment of women in heavy or outdoor work. There was no direct action to force women to leave their work, but it became an unwritten rule in mining communities that when girls married they ceased to work at collieries. Unmarried females were not employed in surface jobs when new pits opened. If they worked at a pit which closed they had to find alternative work. By 1870 it was extremely rare for a woman to be working at a Yorkshire mine other than as a charwoman cleaning the offices.

Miners' wages in Yorkshire were generally better than in other areas and miners' wives were expected to remain at home looking after the family. The census for Jarrett's Building, a tenement built in Worsbrough Dale to house colliery workers, shows that from 1861 until 1911 hardly any miner's wife earned a wage. Those who needed more money than the husband could earn did so by overcrowding their homes with lodgers. This has parallels with the Durham area, where an acceptable way for a miner's widow to obtain an income, and remain in the family home if this was a tied cottage, was to take in as lodgers men who were working at the colliery.

Mining widows and orphans in Yorkshire were supported by the local miners' association if they were in need. In 1866, widows could receive up to 5 shillings a week if their husband lost his life whilst at work and 1 shilling for each child under twelve. Miners subscribed to a fund from their wages to ensure that their families were not left destitute if they were killed at work. This was important because as mining communities developed there were not many ways for an adult woman to earn money.

One of the enduring images of mining women is of anxious waits at the pit-head for news of husbands and sons missing in underground explosions. It is probable that some Barnsley women who had worked underground themselves gathered at Oaks colliery in 1847 and again in 1849, at Edmunds Main in 1862 and at Oaks yet again in 1866.

Esther Day exemplifies the experiences of bereaved wives and mothers. On a winter's morning in February 1842 her second daughter, Mary, never returned from hurrying at the Hopwood pit. On a spring day in March 1847 Esther's husband, Peter, and son, John, died in a huge underground explosion at the Oaks colliery. For hours after the blast the pit hill was crowded with wives, children and friends whose frantic shrieks and wailings were heard at a considerable distance and for a long time wives were lamenting for their husbands and children for their fathers. Esther may have stood amongst this agitated crowd with her two young children and eldest daughter Elizabeth, herself possibly waiting for news of her husband in the rescue party.

Three years later, Esther married another miner, John Depledge. By 1855, her younger son, Peter, was apprenticed to a Sheffield grinder, Joseph Taylor. Following a different trade would have ensured that Peter did not have to risk his life underground even though it meant moving from Barnsley. Taylor was a vicious master but Esther was a woman of spirit. In September 1855, she went to court charging Taylor with assaulting Peter and requesting that his indentures were cancelled. Taylor acknowledged that he had given the lad a savage beating and severely bruised his back but contended that it was appropriate punishment for misbehaviour. The magistrates disagreed and discharged the apprenticeship. Peter returned to work in the pits in Barnsley, grew to adulthood and married. On a bleak December day in 1866, Esther lost a third child underground when Peter perished in another massive explosion at the Oaks colliery, the place where his father and brother had died.

By now the demeanour of mining women at the pit shaft had changed and their grief was no longer expressed through noise. Those who stood watching and waiting were noted to have pale, rigid features and a fixed and tearless gaze trained on the pit shaft. Observers who saw the grieving women recorded that their quiet and dignified demeanour marked a sorrow that was too deep to be expressed and too painful to witness.

Yorkshire was not the only place where women grieved at the pit-head but in parts of Scotland, Wales and Lancashire, some of them forged and maintained roles as workers. The development and survival of pit-brow work for women in any locality was driven by economics. If a large number of females had worked underground, a large number of males were needed to replace them in order to maintain output. In towns and villages without surplus males the workforce needed to rearrange itself if pits were to remain productive.

In 1846, Lord Balcarras' agent, Mr Peace, reckoned that one of the Earl's pits near Wigan was operating at a loss because it had insufficient workers. It had not been able to recruit workers to replace the women who had been excluded and had also lost some men who moved to other pits where women were still allowed to work as though the law had not changed.

In areas of sparse population, the most practical way to maintain capacity was for males who worked on the surface to go underground as drawers and putters. Women then took over some of the work that had been vacated by the men at the pit-head. It was a similar situation to Staffordshire and Cumberland where women had established a presence at the surface earlier in the century.

Women who took this work became known as pit-brow lasses in Lancashire, tip girls in Wales and pit-head women in Scotland. The title was a generic one which covered the wide range of tasks which they were involved with.

The localities where pit-brow women became an established part of the workforce were those which had no alternative industry in 1842. In Lancashire, women were employed around St Helens and Wigan. In Scotland they worked along the upper reaches of the Forth such as Falkirk and Dunfermline and in Fife. In south Wales, female workers were particularly common in the area around Tredeagar.

Initially, pit-head work recruited women who had been excluded from underground. Within a decade, censuses begin to reveal certain characteristics amongst females who chose to work at the pits. The industry was still in a period of transition, but aspects of employment that became established features in Lancashire in later decades were emerging in Scotland by 1851.

In the Halbeath area of Dunfermline, the 1851 census indicates that pit-head work was a role for single women. There was only one married female and she had no children. More than half the girls were under twenty, suggesting that they had not been working in the pits in 1842. Some of these girls were from families that appear to be financially comfortable. Thirteen-year-old Grace Cook was from a family of miners with all eligible members working. Mary Brodie was the daughter of a mine manager and the family had a servant. At the other end of the scale, the district had several families with older female workers who probably had been displaced. Some may have been close to poverty. Ann Wilson supported her widowed mother. Jean Wilson was unmarried and lived alone. Elizabeth Venters was a widow aged forty-three.

❋   ❋   ❋

Censuses for the Ince and Pemberton areas of Lancashire from 1861 to 1891 also show that the majority of pit-brow lasses were from mining families. Typically they were young, unmarried women in their later teens and early twenties. Work at the pit-head was unsuitable for very young girls as they needed to be tall enough to work at screening tables and strong enough to move tubs of coal.

In many families, some daughters worked at the colliery whilst others were in mills or, occasionally, in service. Although there was insufficient alternative work to accommodate all females who needed a wage some places had other industries, providing an element of choice for each girl about what she did.

It is unlikely that the girl herself chose her work. Parents still had a significant say in how a young teenager earned a living and financial considerations were a key part of that decision. In 1865, Margaret Roughly's mother refused to let her leave the pit because it paid more than service. In a letter to *The Times* in 1883 Wigan coal contractor Ellis Lever, claimed that colliers' daughters seldom had any choice about their work as they were sent to the colliery by parents.

In a situation reminiscent of some mining households in 1841, an eighth of the women were from mining families where all able-bodied members worked at the pits. At Pemberton in 1891, fourteen-year-old Alice Tomlinson laboured on the coal pit bank. She lived in a family of eight. Her father and three adult brothers were miners, making it unlikely that Alice's wage was essential for the family's well-being.

In families where girls followed different occupations, it is striking that four times as many pit-brow girls were eldest daughters than younger ones. This suggests that when an elder daughter started work, families needed the higher wage available from the colliery. When a family had several wage-earners it was less necessary for younger daughters to bring in as much as they possibly could and they were allowed to choose between coal work or mill work.

Almost a fifth of the pit-brow lasses were supporting elderly relatives or widowed mothers and another tenth were widows or single mothers who were supporting themselves and their children. Some of the older widows working at the pit-head had daughters in the mills and were possibly keen for their daughters not to follow them into mining.

Although the majority of girls had fathers who were employed at the colliery, a few had a father who was a widower following a different occupation. In 1891, teenagers Sarah Cartwright and Sarah Holland were the eldest daughters of widowers who worked in the mills. They also had younger siblings who needed support. The father of Maggie Miller, another eldest daughter, was an unemployed furniture maker. Girls who were not from mining families may have turned to pit workers to maximise their earnings when the family was in need, rather than from vocational preference.

A tenth of the pit-brow lasses were married. Half of them had no dependent family whilst the others would have had to leave young children with a carer. Over a generation, it appears to have become less acceptable for a married woman with young children to work as this was less common in 1891 than in 1861.

Amongst the female pit-head workers, one group stands out as likely to have exercised a free choice in favour of colliery work. Up to one fifth of them were young, unmarried women who were lodging with families to whom they were not obviously related. The majority were from Lancashire. The coal industry does not appear to have exerted a pull on women from areas that had excluded their labour.

In some families, working at the pit-head was an inheritance that passed through the generations. Dinah Bradbury's seventeen-year-old daughter, Mary Leatherbarrow, worked at the pit-brow in 1861. The Eatock family also had generations of pit-brow lasses. In 1861, married daughter Elizabeth Unsworth was a colliery worker. Thirty years later her daughter Nancy helped to support her mother through pit bank work. In 1901, members of the extended family, widowed Elizabeth Eatock and two of her daughters, were working at a colliery. There are no indications that Elizabeth worked whilst her husband was alive and she may have been given employment by the colliery as part of a culture that saw jobs being made available to colliers' widows who applied for work. It is not known whether she was a pit worker before her marriage.

✳   ✳   ✳

Pit workers started work at six in the morning and worked at least a ten-hour day. For most females their work involved moving coal or sorting it. When tubs of coal arrived at the pit-head they had to be pushed either to the coal hill where they were tipped and left until needed or directly to the screening area where they were sorted and cleaned. The attribute a woman needed to work successfully at the pit-brow was strength as full tubs were heavy to push. Loading coal onto the screening tables with a shovel also demanded stamina. Over time the degree of strength required became less. Mechanical tips were developed, enabling coal to be tipped directly from tubs onto the sorting belts. Chutes allowed the cleaned coal to fall into tubs instead of having to be loaded manually. Mechanisation meant that the strength required from workers was not as great, and by the start of the twentieth century it was considered that although strong, pit women no longer had to have the strength usually associated with a man in order to do the work successfully.

By the 1860s, pit-head work was no longer a woman's job for life. After the women who were displaced from underground work retired, it became unusual for a woman to spend most of her adult life working at a pit. Most pit-brow lasses worked in the role from becoming old enough to go out to work until they married. In many cases the career would be less than ten years.

As the need to move coal with shovels decreased, female workers were mainly involved in the screening process and at some pits screening became an almost exclusively female occupation. Males who worked at screening were often too old or too young to work underground or disabled.

Screeners stood at either side of tables that performed the function of a riddle, as they had gaps in them for dust and tiny pieces of coal to fall through. Using rakes, workers spread the coal, checking its quality and condition. They broke up large lumps of coal and removed any dirt or stone that had been sent up with it. Periodically, the dust that had fallen underneath the screening tables had to be shovelled out, as a build up would eventually prevent the screens working properly.

Working as a screener was not physically as arduous as moving tubs but as it took place in the open air, in all types of weather, it required a hardy type of woman. It also needed someone who could concentrate and who was prepared to remain in the same place for a period of time.

Mechanisation led to the development of screening belts, which moved the coal in front of the workers who had to watch as it went past, spreading it out and identifying any problem rocks that needed breaking or cleaning. In place of raw strength came judgement and initiative, as women had to ensure that the machinery operated safely and to obtain assistance if any breakdown occurred.

After coal had been screened it had to be loaded into wagons ready for dispatch. Women were involved in this work and a worker was expected to be able to load and move twenty wagons a day. Sometimes this involved workers climbing onto the wagons to make sure that the coal was loaded evenly. This form of work became less common for females and by 1900 their work was increasingly confined to the screening belts.

A few women carried out less common tasks. Some greased and maintained coal trucks. Others were pit-head runners or messengers.

✳   ✳   ✳

For almost twenty years after they were banned from underground work, females were accepted as workers at the pit-head with little question. Overt hostility to their presence began to be voiced around 1860. Investigation reports into the deaths of pit-brow women in Staffordshire around this time comment that the work the woman was engaged in was not a suitable occupation and should be banned to females.

The Lancashire cotton industry suffered badly as a consequence of the American Civil War in the early 1860s, when supplies of raw cotton became scarce as a result of blockades of the ports of the cotton-producing states. Unemployment amongst cotton workers soared, leading to high costs of relieving distress. Mills that were unable to work had no need for coal to power them.

When a man's ability to make a living was challenged, the right of women to work in occupations which men saw as suitable for themselves was questioned. Workers' associations received complaints about women employed at the pit-head. In 1863, the National Miners' Association passed a resolution at its conference in Leeds, calling on Parliament to take steps to end the practice of female employment on the pit banks as it degraded the future mothers of the mining population.

The attitude of some miners towards women workers fits with the emphasis of early union activity in a number of trades. Skilled men tried to restrict the labour supply in order to maintain and improve their own wages. This included trying to impose requirements that workers must be time-served craftsmen before they could work in a trade and that the number of apprenticeships should be restricted. Mining was not a craft industry and it was impractical to attempt to exclude groups of unskilled males whose labour was needed underground to move coal if the output of the hewers was to be maximised. Females, whose interests were neither recognised nor represented, were an easy target for restricting the labour supply and increasing opportunities for male employment.

The proposer of the resolution came from Barnsley, an area firmly against female work at pits, and discussion of the proposal was slight. A delegate who asked what would happen to the large number of girls thrown out of employment was dismissed with derisory laughter and told that they would have to do the same as the women who had been shut out of underground work.

In 1866, a parliamentary committee was appointed to inquire into the operation of the laws for regulating and inspecting mines. By this time, the Mines Act of 1842 had been joined by an act of 1850, which had established formal inspection of mines and an act of 1860, which had strengthened the inspection system and introduced weighmen, who were appointed by the miners to check the weight of coal sent to the surface and ensure that they received the correct payment.

Part of the inquiry covered the work of women at the pit-head. Opponents argued that the work degraded them, made them unfit mothers and led to immorality. The committee heard from witnesses, but found no evidence to support ill-defined allegations of indecency amongst pit women, and when it reported in 1867, members concluded that female employment did not require legislative prohibition or further interference. Whilst opposition remained, the question of banning women from pit-head work slipped into the background for several years.

❅   ❅   ❅

Women engaged in pit-head work had aroused the interest of a much wider population than the miners by the 1860s. The interest may have been stimulated in part by newspaper reports and calls to ban their work. The women in the Wigan area were particularly fascinating because, unlike women in other areas, they wore trousers to work. To meet the demands of the curious visitor, enterprising photographers persuaded a number of pit women to pose in their trousered working clothes in photographers' studios. The pictures were then sold as post cards.

Photographs of pit women from this period are a fascinating but imperfect record. Those taken in studio surroundings show women posing in romanticised settings alongside trappings of their work such as shovels and riddles. The pictures appear artificial and fail to give any impression of the model or the reality of her toil. For some, the visit to the studio would have been an alien experience and one the woman agreed to because of the inducement of a few pennies for a modelling fee.

Some photographers visited pits and took pictures of women at their places of work. Some are of posed groups whilst others purport to show them working. These are also artificial, and often show workers posing for a photograph whilst pretending to work rather than revealing the nature of that labour. They are most useful in recording the age profile of the women and the development of their working attire and places of work.

Within a ten mile radius of Wigan pit-women's working clothes usually consisted of a shirt, said to be blue-striped, a waistcoat, trousers that were topped by a short skirt and perhaps an apron also. They wore sturdy boots and a bonnet or scarf to protect their hair from dust and dirt. In other areas of Lancashire, Scotland, Staffordshire and Wales they wore skirts that ended a few inches above the ankle.

As the century progressed, their clothes became more feminine whilst remaining practical. Photographs and contemporary descriptions show that they wore brightly-coloured accessories such as shawls, scarves and hats. Although Wigan women were sometimes reported to be almost indistinguishable from men the only times this was likely to be the case was when they were glimpsed from a distance as they wore jackets that had been cast off by fathers and brothers. The rest of the time they were unmistakably female, although their appearance was not that of conventional femininity.

To a mid-Victorian, Wigan's trousered pit-brow lasses would have appeared an exotic species, as interesting to the intellectual mind as the plants and animals being gathered from faraway destinations and put on display in zoological and botanical gardens. For the less intellectual, the unusual appearance of the women would have provided a frisson of the voyeurism associated with the peep shows and freak shows that were popular attractions in the pleasure parks of the time. It was a similar frisson to that provoked by half-naked figures in the woodcuts of 1842.

A Victorian gentleman whose interest in working-class women sprang from a genuine wish to understand them and their lives was civil servant, Arthur Munby. For most of his adult life Munby kept diaries and notebooks recording a wealth of detail about women whose jobs involved hard, physical graft. Coal was one of these occupations and he visited pits around Wigan several times and spoke to women who worked there. He was invited into the homes of some of them to discover how they lived when they were not at work. He recorded his recollections of the conversations he had with them, sketched them in their local surroundings and persuaded some of them to pose for photographs in their working clothes.

Munby's records confirm the findings of the Royal Commission that mining girls lacked formal education and many were rough and ready in their speech and ways. They belie any suggestion that they were coarse, uncouth or immoral. At work they coped with tasks that were physically hard and made their faces and hands black and grimy. Away from the pit they were clean, bonny women who wore conventional dresses and skirts and were capable of carrying out their domestic role to the same standards as other working women, capable of aspiring to the same dreams cherished by other working-class girls. In 1873, when a special correspondent for the *Guardian* produced some reports from the mining areas of Lancashire he noted that pit girls, duly cleaned up and well-presented, were some of the biggest purchasers of sheet-music in the Wigan area.

The debate about whether pit-head work was suitable for women gained fresh impetus around 1883 with Ellis Lever's letter in *The Times*. He claimed that the job brutalised the natures of men and women and led to an undesirable situation in which women became breadwinners and men shirked their duties to maintain their families.

Although Lever gave a middle-class perspective, lamenting the dearth of domestic servants and pointing out that women could take on this work, working miners and their associations were sympathetic to the view that lasses had no place at the pit-head. The1880s had as its backdrop declining prosperity, as other countries began to haul in the early industrial advantage that Britain had established. Decreased trade translated into reduced employment and lower wages and men again became more vocal about jobs that they thought should be theirs by right. Manoeuvring women out of pit-head work was a way of protecting male employment.

The debate fractured into two streams of thought. Alleged immorality amongst pit women and the unsuitable nature of the work continued to be the focus of opposition from miners and their representatives. Immorality was an accusation which was difficult to define or disprove. It is likely that it still hurt women as much as it had in 1842 when, after their exclusion, a Lancashire female miner had asked why women working at collieries were considered to have lesser standards than those who worked in factories.

Immorality may have stuck in the minds of miners after the parliamentary investigation of 1867 concluded that there was no evidence of this, because of the stature of Frederick Engels who had collaborated with Karl Marx on the Communist Manifesto. As a leading socialist thinker, his study of the working classes in England in 1844 attained a status that would not normally be associated with such a time-specific piece of writing. Although it was not published in translation until 1887, those interested in such matters knew its contents and were able to disseminate them in discussions.

Engels' approach in this study is now recognised as flawed as he failed to ensure that examples he used were accurate and balanced. His information about miners was largely based on the Commission report. As had been feared in 1841 by those concerned about what the Commissioners would conclude, Engels extracted the worst examples and presented them as representative of the whole. He portrayed women as half-crippled by their work, prone to dying in labour, producing more illegitimate children than other working women and working almost naked below ground. It is not surprising that some working men persisted in their belief that women's employment at coal mines degraded the status of the working-class as a whole.

By the 1880s, the middle-classes had moved away from accusations which can be traced back to the 1842 report. Their sensibilities baulked at superficialities or matters which inconvenienced them. Opponents of female pit workers condemned as unsuitable the clothes which pit-women wore, concerned that dirt and trousers might somehow corrupt the women or those who observed them in that unsexed state. Whether the work was too heavy for any female, or prevented them looking after their families properly, was of little concern.

Against a background of agitation from the Miners' Association, a proposal to exclude women from pit-head work was included in the Mines Bill of 1887. Middle-class public opinion decisively rounded on the narrow-mindedness of critics who condemned the women's attire. Newspapers pointed out the hypocrisy of those who pronounced the pit clothes worn by women as indecent whilst being silent about the revealing costumes worn by the ballet dancer, the pantomime fairy and prosperous women attending evening parties and banquets. It was noted that Turkish and Chinese women wore trousers and that educated women were promoting them as acceptable female clothing. A consensus developed that dress should be accommodated to occupations rather than honest women being denied honest work because their dress offended the sensibilities of the pretentious. The press made little attempt to specify what was meant by honest work and the points about suitability that were made by working men were not well-addressed in their pages.

In the Lancashire area, women received much support. In 1885, a mines inspector reported that they had been gratuitously libelled and that he found them orderly and hard-working. Almost as soon as the clause proposing exclusion was published high profile supporters began to promote the women's cause in public meetings and correspondence with newspapers. Reverend Harry Mitchell of Pemberton identified 160 pit women in his parish of whom 133 were single and in need of their wage. Wigan's mayoress, Margaret Park, wrote and spoke in favour of the women and helped to organise a deputation to London to lobby the Home Secretary.

In May 1887, twenty-two pit women went to London accompanied by male colleagues, coal owners, Margaret Park and Reverend Mitchell. Some wore their working clothes as they paraded to Parliament. The event had an air of celebration as the women publicly demonstrated that they were healthy and feminine, even in their working attire. The meeting with the Home Secretary, Henry Matthews, may have been an anti-climax as, without having to argue their case, they were told that the controversial clause was to be removed.

The views of many of the pit women at this time were not well-recorded. It was reported that they were reluctant to attend public meetings and did not speak on their own behalf. Although their supporters stressed the right of a woman to select how she earned a living, it is likely that what concerned many of the women was the lack of any suitable alternative employment rather than an overwhelming desire to work at the pit-head. Whilst Ellis Lever reported that there were ample vacancies for servants others pointed out that the rough and ready ways of mining girls made it likely that the only employers who would consider them for the role were rough public houses.

✳   ✳   ✳

By 1887, it had been acknowledged that pit-head work was healthy. It was not necessarily safe. Between 1851 and 1913 an average of two women's deaths per year have been identified, forty-eight in Lancashire, forty-five in Scotland and twenty-three in Wales. Deaths also occurred in Cumberland, the Midlands and Yorkshire though on a much smaller scale. Almost all the deaths would now be considered avoidable as they could have been prevented by designing and enforcing safe systems of working.

The first recorded death of a female at a pit after 1842 was cryptically cited by Engels as evidence that the Mines Act was ineffective. It occurred at Wigan in January 1844 when seventeen-year-old Margaret Wignall took her father's lunch to the pit and then went to peer down the shaft. She was told to stand back by the foreman, which she did but almost immediately walked forward again, hastily wrapped her petticoat round her legs and, to the consternation of those around, jumped into the pit. No reason for her suicide was discovered.

A mine was a complex industrial operation and working there exposed a woman to a wide range of risks. Wagons of some sort feature in the majority of deaths. Workers were crushed between a moving wagon and another object. They were knocked down and run over by trucks, which were heavy when loaded with coal. Some were hit when trucks which were being hoisted were suddenly lowered without warning. In Lancashire trucks were implicated in the deaths of thirty-four women. In Wales they were responsible for sixteen and in Scotland seventeen.

A few women were crushed as they dodged between trucks as they moved round the site. A number of those crushed by wagons were let down by the men manoeuvring them who failed to check whether it was safe to move them or who did not shout safety warnings. Margaret Gore was told to come down from a wagon she was loading so that it could be shunted but not given enough time to do so and fell as it moved off. Her arm was badly crushed as the wagon rolled over it. She died from complications arising from an operation to amputate it a few days later.

In 1913, thirty-one-year-old Mary Hogg died when the boy who was assisting her signalled to the engineman that she was clear when she was still involved in loading the cage. Although safety had been considered, a system that relied on the judgement of an inexperienced youngster would now be considered to be inadequate.

More than a fifth of the deaths in Scotland and Wales were the result of women falling into the mine. In Swansea in 1853, Sarah Morris fell down the pit shaft when she was dazzled by a pit lamp. In 1856, Helen Snaddon of Falkirk slipped into the pit shaft whilst pushing a coal tub towards it. This type of accident was most prevalent in the early part of the period. By the 1870s, more attention had been given to pit-head fencing, following legislation designed to make pits safer.

Falls in Lancashire were of a different type and involved hazards on the surface. There were proportionately less of them than in the other areas, indicating the more developed nature of Lancashire's mines in the mid-century. In 1880, Mary Catterall was found drowned in the colliery's canal. The reason for her being there was not identified. In 1882, Ellen Taylor, a fifteen-year-old screener from Wigan, fell into a tank of hot water whilst filling her can. Thirty years later the cover of a well of hot water gave way beneath Margaret Chapman's feet. Both women died from scalding.

Clothes were the root cause of several deaths. This was much more frequent in Scotland and Wales than in Lancashire which suggests that the Lancashire practice of wearing trousers contributed to a woman's safety. There were far fewer trailing hems that could become entangled in machinery. Three deaths in Lancashire involved clothing. In Scotland there were eight.

A few deaths were the results of less predictable accidents. At the Fordel colliery in 1876, Ellen Cook, Isobel Harrover, Catherine Penman and Isobel Philip were amongst the victims of a boiler explosion. In 1871 at Wigan, Alice Hackett died from a wound to her leg from a fork.

Safety appears to have improved markedly by the twentieth century and negligent managers could feel the force of the law. When Mary Prescott's clothes caught in machinery in 1902 the manager was convicted for not ensuring that it was fenced off. A higher number of deaths in this period may have resulted from the contributory negligence by the victims. In separate incidents Georgina Wilson, Jeannie McGhee and Mary Lynch ignored safety procedures. Georgina was taking a short-cut home through a shunting area when she was hit by trucks although a safe route had been provided for workers. It is not known why Jeannie and Mary ignored fences. They became entangled in machinery.

Fatal accidents were only the tip of the ice-berg. There would have been several times as many accidents resulting in serious injury. Margaret Bisset's leg had to be amputated after a wagon ran over it. An amputated or mangled limb was more than a source of personal distress, it affected a woman's ability to earn a living or to look after her family.

Susan McFarlane was off work for three months after being struck by a safety gate and Mary Kyle for a similar period after a wagon set off unexpectedly. Martha Currie was far luckier. She only took two days off work when her hand was crushed by a pinion wheel.

✻　✻　✻

Although pit-head work remained open to women in 1887, hostility from working men did not go away. The most prominent opponents of women in mining were the miners' associations. The hostility was part of a wider working-class male view about what was women's work. The view held by many was that women's work was anything men did not wish to do. Very little consideration was given to how women who needed to earn a living should do so in areas that were not well-provisioned with alternatives. Some of the arguments used against women at the pit-head said little for the men who made them. It was argued that excluding women would prevent them being exposed to bad language, not taking into account that those who exposed then to bad language were the men themselves. In 1893, Mines Inspector Henry Hall stated in his report for Lancashire, that the reformers who were trying to prevent the employment of women at the pit-head could spend their energies more usefully in trying to abate the nuisance of the dreadful language used by young miners underground, describing it as a babel of oaths.

Despite the policy opposition of the Miners' Association to females in the industry it did allow women to join the union and was prepared to support their interests as workers until exclusion was achieved. Union officials advocated that, like men, females should be eligible for compensation for injuries sustained at work. Who the female union members were is unclear but it is likely that they were adult women, perhaps wives, daughters or sisters of men who were actively involved in union activities. Some women may have been interested in politics or may have witnessed the benefits that union support could bring to working men and, by extension, to their families. In April 1873, a miners' conference heard that, after a strike in Wales, which lasted for three months, women became passionate advocates of union membership and many requested that they should be allowed to join. At that time their request was not taken seriously.

According to research carried out in 1920 by Fabian Society member Barbara Drake, female membership of the the Miners' Union increased from 290 in 1896 to 1,041 by 1914. Members were found across all the coalfields where women worked. Although numerically low this was not an insignificant proportion at a time when the number of females working in the industry was around 6,000.

The final attempt to exclude women from coal mines, before the Great War created a need for women to replace men in a variety of occupations, took place in 1911. Once again this coincided with a period of economic hardship for workers as prices were rising faster than wages. Following agitation from miners' representatives, a clause to phase out female employment was inserted into the Mines Bill during its committee stage. Women already working were to be allowed to continue but no further women would be employed. The exclusion clause provoked another strong campaign by the pit-brow women of Lancashire and their supporters. Amongst them was the Labour MP for Ince, Stephen Walsh, who opposed his party and his union colleagues. A former miner, he had worked alongside pit women and understood the nature of their work and the reasons why they adopted the occupation.

Walsh supported only the woman's right to work at the pit-head. He strenuously denied that pit women were degraded by their work, but he did not acknowledge that the work was suitable for females and would have preferred other and better opportunities for employment to be available to them. In his speeches he identified that in the Wigan area there were scarcely any factories, there was no work in the fields and that few people employed domestic servants. He considered that poverty, rather than any firm liking for the work, was the reason women continued to be attracted to work at coal mines.

As in 1887 the committee's amendment sparked rallies in favour of the women. A petition was organised and around fifty women and their supporters travelled to London and marched to the Houses of Parliament where they met the Home Secretary. In terms of advancing the women's cause the meeting was unnecessary. The amendment by the committee had been made against the advice and wishes of the government, and the delegation received assurances that it would be overturned when the bill returned to the House of Commons for its third reading.

The debate that took place in the House of Commons in December 1911 when government minister Charles Masterman proposed that the amendment to ban women should be reversed shows how the role of the government had developed since 1842. Ashley had to fight as an individual for legislation to protect females as regulating the conditions of workers was not seen as a subject on which a government should take a view. Two generations later the government actively supported the cause of mining women as part of a bill that placed more regulations of the industry.

Even in 1911, the debates of summer 1842 were still in the minds of some MPs. Llewellyn Atherley-Jones pointed out the irony that the argument that a woman had the right to decide for herself whether the pit was an acceptable place for her to earn her living had been derided and condemned in 1842 when owners made the same point.

The Labour Party, with the high-profile exception of Stephen Walsh, was closely linked to the union movement and supported the exclusion clause. The proffered reason was that they wanted to see women protected from a degrading occupation that was not worthy of the civilisation of the twentieth century. Although assertions of immorality had been made earlier in the year by miners' leaders, parliamentarians of all parties held back from this suggestion in their discussions and went out of their way to stress that pit-brow lasses were decent, honest and moral women. Seventy years after the moral standards of mining women had first been dragged into official disrepute, Parliament publicly acknowledged that the allegation was without truth.

With immorality, like clothing a generation earlier, no longer an assertion that could command serious discussion, the opposition to women working at the pit-head focused on an economic issue, the wages of the working man and the belief that women were responsible for low wages. Women earned less than 2 shillings a day whilst men working at the pit-heads in the areas where women did not work were paid up to 5 shillings. Although gender disparity of wages was a fact of working life at the time, in some instances the wages of teenage girls were being compared to those of adult men. Some MPs doubted the arguments that women were the cause of low wages, pointing out that if they were dismissed, those replacing them would be unskilled workers or boys who would not have substantially higher earning power for the work that had to be done. Sir George Toulmin suggested that if women were being exploited by low wages the unions could become involved in ensuring that they received adequate remuneration.

In 1911, suffragette campaigns for women to have the vote meant that the issue of women's rights was politically very high profile. The need for some women to earn a wage to maintain themselves was now understood. Stephen Walsh argued that if any form of work was barred to women there should be other suitable and appropriately paid work available locally. Miners in Staffordshire thought that women should be allowed to continue in their work as there were no other jobs available. Working men in some areas supported the right of their wives and daughters to work at the pit-head. Influential opinion was not likely to agree that it was acceptable to deprive women of the means of making a living by imposing on them the views of men who lived and worked in other areas that their job was not a socially acceptable way for a female to earn her keep.

On behalf of the government, Charles Masterman argued that only three conditions could justify excluding women from any line of work. If it was not corrupting their morals, damaging their health or wearing them down by its oppressive nature the choice should remain with the woman.

There was no evidence that pit lasses were immoral or corrupted. It was accepted that women were exposed to bad language from men but this was seen as the fault of the men and one that the women should not be penalised for.

There was ample testimony from doctors in Lancashire that the work was healthy and those who opposed women at the pit-head were unable to identify any female whose health had been damaged by the exertions. Although names were not given, supporters were able to cite examples of girls in poor health leaving factories and regaining their vitality by working outdoors. Doctors had recommended pit-brow work rather than factory work for many years for females who suffering from anaemia and respiratory complaints.

No evidence was produced that women were being worn down by the work. Atherley-Jones felt that it was degrading for a soot-blackened woman to return to her home and family in that condition. He said that countless mining communities across the country had imposed local rules that women did not work at pits. Parliament should now complete for two dark, forgotten corners of the earth the work that public opinion had begun elsewhere. The counter-argument was that individual mining communities could decide what was acceptable for their own locality but had no right to impose their views on communities that did not share them.

After a lively and wide-ranging debate the amendment made in committee was removed by a majority of more than four to one. Once again, women remained free to continue to work at the pit-head in the areas where social conditioning had not rendered it unacceptable. For those dependent on pit work for their livelihood, it was an early Christmas present.

*　　*　　*

One of the more surprising aspects of the lives of nineteenth-century mining women is consistency. Their role was shaped over the decades by the level of economic development in the local mining industry and the availability of alternative means of earning a living. At the start of the century the quality of coal being mined locally determined whether a female had a role in mining. A pit owner's need to maximise his profits from any investment to extract coal from deep seams was the economic driver that removed females from underground work. After 1842 this would have continued under its own momentum, irrespective of the Mines Act.

In places where a variety of industries developed incomers arrived to seek work. Any influx of males led to women being displaced from work in mines and taking jobs in alternative occupations. If no industries developed to draw in a newer population, local mining economies tended to rearrange themselves spontaneously with women taking roles at the pithead whilst men worked underground.

When localities grew a little more prosperous, and men were able to maintain a family on their own wage, social factors became as important as economic ones and public opinion began to determine whether a female could have any role at a pit. Even without the impetus provided by the Mines Act the underlying economic and social conditions make it probable that females in Yorkshire would have abandoned pit work within a generation, joining Northumberland and Cumberland, where this change had already taken place.

The changing role of women at coal mines was accelerated in 1842 by legislation that abruptly altered the work which a female could legally undertake. The consequence of the Children's Employment Commission Report of 1842 was that middle-class opinion laid down a marker about what type of work was socially acceptable for women, after eleven horrified men acted as the moral jury of the country, suggesting that there was a line that unfettered economics should not be allowed to cross.

The Mines and Collieries Act was an imperfect response to the sub-Commissioners' horror. Although the act restricted how women were permitted to earn their living it did nothing to change the economic development of localities or ensure that suitable other work was available to them. Local resistance to the Mines Act arose because of the imposition of a social solution to an economic question without acknowledging or addressing the problems caused for some of those affected by the change.

Had the Mines Act not been passed the introduction or growth of new industries in areas not developed in 1842 would have gradually provided opportunities for females to leave the industry. This would probably have been welcomed by owners and hewers who realised that adolescent males were better equipped to maximise production. It would have been welcomed by many women, few of whom hankered after hard graft in a colliery. Pit-head work was not an occupation of choice but an occupation of necessity for a significant proportion of pit-brow women, and their opposition to changes that threatened their livelihood arose from concern about losing a source of income that they could not replace rather than on any liking for the work.

It is unlikely that women would have retained a substantial role underground by the end of the century even without legislation. Efforts to maximise productivity would have quickly removed young girls from the work and adult women over time as the superior physical strength of adolescent males would have proved more beneficial in moving heavy coal tubs.

Few women had a choice about whether they worked as miners in 1800 and this was also the case at the turn of the next century. If a female's family needed her to maximise their income she had to follow their wishes and work at the mine in whatever role was permitted to her.

Throughout the century, mining females were little different from any other working women. Whilst strength was frequently associated with them and their clothing was strange, outside work they were clean and well presented and possessed the same level of domestic and parenting skills as those women who worked in mills and factories.

The most startling aspect of similarity across a century is the number of females involved in mining. From 1841, whenever the number of females was discussed the number remained around 6,000. In 1911, this comprised 2,700 in Scotland, 2,500 in Lancashire and around 800 in Staffordshire, along with a few in isolated locations where the weight of public opinion had not succeeded in stamping the practice out.

Compared with 1841 it reveals remarkable consistency. The figures for Scotland are almost identical although the geographical area where women worked was smaller. The numbers for Staffordshire are not greatly reduced. In Lancashire, where the coal industry had expanded, the number of women had also increased, though as a proportion of the numbers employed in the industry they had declined. The main change was that within the total number, the age range was narrower as the workforce no longer included young girls or elderly women.

The nineteenth century was a period of remarkable social and industrial change in which the British coal industry grew, and improved its mining practices to meet the hungry demands of a manufacturing nation. A complex industrial economy grew rich on the fuel that coal provided and then began to decline. Sucessive generations of women who lived in mining families experienced identical worries as they watched their men set out to get their living in a highly dangerous occupation. And coal itself, the black as night source of heat, power and wealth, maintained throughout these years a very direct and powerful hold over a similar number of female workers.

The Number of Female Miners in 1841

Official Census Figures

	women 20+ years	women under 20	Total women
England and Wales	789	794	1,583
Scotland	396	371	767
Total	1,185	1,165	2,350

This is not the first research to notice that the number of female miners recorded in the 1841 census is considerably less than the number included in employers' returns to the Children's Employment Commission a few months earlier.

Previous attempts to identify a more realistic total have not been well-publicised, and the figure of 2,350 that was widely disseminated by Engels, is the one which immediately comes to light for anyone trying to discover how many women and girls were employed in mining in 1842.

I had already produced my own analysis by the time I discovered other work on the subject. This confirmed my conclusion that there was likely to have been around 6,000 female miners affected by the Mines Act. I have not seen any detail of how others arrived at their total. The following summarises my reasoning.

Children's Employment Commission Reports

	Adults	13–18 years	under 13 years	Total
East Scotland				
Mid-Lothian	341	189	54	
Peebleshire	17	7	13	
East Lothian	109	95	35	
West Lothian	65	52	37	
Stirlingshire	212	120	99	
Perthshire	157	165	68	
Dunfermline – St Andrews	305	181	57	
Total c/f	1,206	809	363	2,378

b/f	1,206	809	363	2,378

Lancashire
(extracted from Appendix A)   365   315   114   794

Yorkshire 1
(extracted from Appendix B)   86   139   164   389

South Wales
(Returns to Jones)

Pembrokeshire	132	37	6	
(personally visited by Franks)				
Glamorganshire	45	43	27	
Monmouthshire	1	4	1	
Glamorganshire	5	2	1	
Carmarthenshire	262	49	–	
Pembrokeshire (est)	18	12	1	
Total	463	147	36	646

Grand total   **4,207**

Across the country, returns from employers were not complete and may have been inaccurate. In Scotland, Franks felt the figures he included were substantially accurate after corrections he had made but he noted that some returns (his tables suggest about fifteen) had not been received.

The first inspection report produced by Tremenheere in 1844 covered this area and identified higher numbers of females than had been included in the returns and one colliery that did not feature of Franks' list. The difference between Tremenheere's figures and those of Franks, for three pits where substantial understatement in 1841 appears likely, is 128. Tremenheere visited only a small number of the collieries recorded by Franks raising the possibility of similar understatements elsewhere.

Eighty-two females were discovered by Tancred in West Scotland. Tremenheere's Report indicates that one mine may have understated the number in 1841 by twenty.

Many owners in Lancashire did not provide any returns and some of those who sent in figures may have provided inaccurate ones. In view of the number of women reportedly working in Lancashire mines, this county's figure is likely to have been substantially under-stated.

No tabulated data was included in the Yorkshire 2 report. Wood had received returns indicating that 1,667 children and young people were employed but he did not analyse this in terms of gender. He commented that many returns had not been received and he estimated that the total would be double if all returns were made. Assuming that the figure was 3,300, if an eighth were female this would add around 400 to the total. Within the witness statements and tables, twenty-four girls can be identified.

Symons appears to have included just the returns he received. It is not possible to identify the extent of missing data.

In Wales, Franks only provided figures for the collieries he visited. Rhys Jones, who had received some returns, found that many owners refused to co-operate in providing information.

A number of the Welsh mines were co-located with iron works. Some females recorded at iron works may have been engaged in mining.

Small numbers of women and girls were working in other areas. A few were noted in Cumberland and North Lancashire. Higher though unspecified numbers were referred to in Staffordshire and North Wales in surface occupations

It is likely that some women worked when they were needed rather than every week. As returns were made at a point in time they were unlikely to include anyone not at work at that point.

Trying to adjust for the amount of the various understatements adds little value. The definitive data available, and knowledge of where understatement is likely to have occurred, suggests that around 6,000 females were involved in mining in 1841 and likely to be affected by the Mines Act of 1842.

Commission witnesses traced to the 1841 census beyond reasonable doubt

The number in brackets is the witness statement in the relevant report. Names followed by * indicate identification confirmed by descendent/ relative.

Lancashire (Kennedy)
Eliza and Mary Ann Hunt (20, 21)
Mary Glover (26)
Margaret Winstanley (36)
Betty Houghton (39)
Jane Sym (72)
Dinah Bradbury* (73)
Rosa Lucas (92)

Scotland (Franks)
Alison Adam (12)
Janet Borrowman (218)
Jesse Coutte (118)
Ann Crookston (101)
Margaret Crookston (141)
Margaret Drysdale (49)
Phyllis Flockhart (11)
Agnes Fuller (Fowler) (58)
Margaret Harper (189)
Margaret Hervie (190)
Isabel Hugh (416)
Ellison (Alison) Jack (55)
Margaret Jaques (Jack) (25)
Catherine Landels (165)
Margaret Leveston (Livingstone) (116)
Elizabeth Litster (417)
Elizabeth M'Neil (136)
Martha M'Neil (139)

Mary MacQueen (54)
Catherine Meiklejohn (164)
Agnes Moffatt (23)
Janet Moffatt (70)
Mary Neilson (119)
Jane Peacock Watson (117)
Elizabeth Pentland (60)
Agnes Reid (2)
Helen Reid (26)
Janet Selkirk (109)
Elizabeth Selkirk (111)
Mary Sneddon (219)
Helen Spowort (355)
Helen Spowort (358)
Margaret Watson (115)
Helen Weir (342)
Janet Welsh (415)
Isabel Wilson (134)

South Wales (Franks)
Hannah Bowen (422)
Hester Callan (452)
Eliza Prout (451)
Susan Reece (48)

South Wales (Jones)
Margaret Morgan (162)

Yorkshire (Scriven)
Ann Ambler (1)

Mary and Ruth Barratt (72, 73)
Esther and Harriet Craven* (75, 76)
Margaret Gormley (9)
Anna Hoile (70)
Patience Kershaw (26)
Susan Pitchforth (10)

Yorkshire (Wood)
Mary Ann Lund (70)

Yorkshire (Symons)
Matilda Carr (102)
Hannah Clarkson (104)
Elizabeth and Mary Day (85, 89)
Fanny Drake (206)

Ann and Elizabeth Eggley* (113, 114)
Ann Fern (136b)
Ann, Maria, and Sarah Gooder (117, 112, 116)
Ann and Mary Hague (39, 40)
Ann Hinchcliffe (286)
Ann Hollings (105)
Mary Holmes (283)
Harriet Morton (38)
Caroline Swallow (292)
Rachel Tinker* (285)
Margaret Westwood (192)

There are some practical difficulties in identifying witnesses on the 1841 census:

- variable spelling of surnames (Hoile or Hoyle);
- nicknames (Elizabeth or Betty);
- uncertainty about age;
- rounding down to the nearest five years of adult ages in the 1841 census;
- very common names, often specific to localities;
- transcription errors.

The number of girls identified in Yorkshire is a tribute to the interviewing skills of Samuel Scriven and Jellinger Symons and to the recording by their clerks. These sub-Commissioners elicited detail about families that proved invaluable.

In tracing the subsequent lives of the witnesses additional difficulties arise:

- Insufficient information within the GRO indexes to identify marriages and deaths.
- Geographic mobility between census periods.

Weights and Measures in Nineteenth-Century Britain

Money

Money was made up of pounds (£), shillings (s) and pence (d). The sign £ was placed before the number. The signs s and d were placed after the number.

£1 = 20s
1s = 12d

A penny divided into half pennies and farthings (a farthing was a quarter of a penny). The sum of 2s 6d was known as half a crown. As a comparator in modern currency 5p is 1 shilling. £1 in 1840 was worth £44.10 in 2005.

Measurement

Weights were ton (ton), hundredweight (cwt), stone (st), pound (lb), ounce (oz).

20 cwt = 1 ton
8 st = 1 cwt
14 lb = 1 st
16 oz = 1 lb

As a comparator, 1 kilogram is approximately 2lb 2oz.

Distances were mile (ml), yard (yd), foot (ft) and inch (in).

1 ml = 1,760 yds
1 yd = 3 ft
1 ft = 12 ins

As a comparator 1 metre is approximately 1 yard and 3 inches.

In the text, measurements of less than 1d or 1 included in primary sources have been rounded to the nearest whole unit (½ has been rounded down).

Glossary of Mining Terms

Air-door boy/girl – Worker who opens and closes ventilation doors (Wales).

Bank – Outdoor storage area for coal.

Bearer – Person who carries coal on their back (Scotland).

Crail – Basket in which coal is carried on the back.

Corve – Container used to move coal (Yorkshire).

Drawer – Worker who moves coal underground (Lancashire).

Face – Place from where coal is cut underground.

Getter – Miner who hews coal.

Hewer – Miner who hews coal.

Hurrier – Worker who pulls coal trucks underground (Yorkshire).

Pumper – Worker who pumps water from wet pits.

Putter – Worker who moves coal underground (Scotland).

Riddler – Worker who sieves dust out of coal.

Thruster – Worker who pushes coal trucks underground (Yorkshire).

Trammer – Worker who moves coal underground.

Trapper – Worker who opens and closes ventilation doors.

Wagon – Tub in which coal is moved.

Winder – Worker who operates winding gear.

Sources and Bibliography

Primary sources

Annual Reports of the Commissioner of Mines 1844–50
Census Returns 1841–1901
Hansard June–August 1842
Report of the Children's Employment Commission 1842 (Mines and Collieries) and its appendices
Report of the Factory Commission 1833
Report of the Sanitary Commission 1842
The Times
The Manchester Guardian
The Morning Chronicle

Secondary sources

Boyd Hilton, *The New Oxford History of England, A Mad, Bad and Dangerous People England 1783–1846*, Clarenden Press, 2006.
Engels, Frederick, *The Condition of the Working Clasees in England in 1844*, 1845 (translated into English 1887), Penguin Classics, 2006.
John, Angela V, *By the Sweat of their Brow, Women Workers at Victorian Coal Mines*, 1984.
Kirkby, Peter, 'Child Labour, Public Decency and the Iconography of the Children's Employment Commission 1842' in *Manchester Papers in Economic and Social History*, No 62, 2007.
Mathias, Peter, *The First Industrial Nation, The Economic History of Britain 1700–1914*, Routledge, 2001 (first published in 1969).
Hammond, J L and Hammond B, *The Town Labourer 1760–1832*, Alan Sutton, 1995 (first published by Longman in 1917).
Hammond J L and Hammond B, *Lord Shaftesbury*, Penguin, 1939 (first published 1923)
Hodder, E, *Lord Shaftesbury*, 1888.
Hoppen, Theodore K, *The New Oxford History of England – The Mid-Victorian Generation, 1846–1886*, Oxford University press, 2000 (first published in 1998).
Thompson, E P, *The Making of the English Working Class*, Victor Gollancz, 1980 (first published 1963).
Dictionary of National Biography.

Websites

A Vision of Britain through Time – www.visionofbritain.org.uk
Coal Mining History Resources Centre – www.cmhrc.co.uk
Women and the Pits – http://freepages.genealogy.rootsweb.ancestry.com
Scottish Mining – www.scottishmining.co.uk
Pit Brow Lasses Scrapbook (Dave Lane) – www.daveweb.co.uk

Details about female miners

Dinah Bradbury, Esther and Harriet Craven, Elizabeth Day, Ann and Elizabeth Eggley, Sarah Gooder, Rachel Tinker and Rebecca Whitehead – researched or corroborated by family history researchers.

Patience Wroe – 'A Yorkshire Pit Lass' by Elsie Green, in the *Barnsley Family History Society Journal*, 1994.

Rebecca Melling – *Manchester Guardian*, 27 January, 8 February and 24 April 1844.

Margaret Wignall – *Manchester Guardian*, 8 February 1844.

Jane Moss – *Manchester Guardian*, 2 December 1846.

Esther Depledge (Day) – *Barnsley Times* 8 September 1855.

Further Reading

Davies, Alan, *The Pit Brow Women of the Wigan Coalfield*, The History Press, 2006 (an illustrated account of female colliery surface workers in the Wigan area of Lancashire).

Gallop, Alan, *Victoria's Children of the Dark*, The History Press, 2010 (previously published as *Children of the Dark* in 2003 (a detailed study of the Huskar Pit disaster).

John, Angela, *By the Sweat of their Brow, Women Workers at Victorian Coal Mines* (a more detailed study of pit-brow lasses in the later part of the nineteenth century), Routledge, 1984 (new edition).

Index